Arthur Johnson Evans

A Primer of Free Church History

Arthur Johnson Evans

A Primer of Free Church History

ISBN/EAN: 9783743330405

Manufactured in Europe, USA, Canada, Australia, Japa

Cover: Foto ©Lupo / pixelio.de

Manufactured and distributed by brebook publishing software (www.brebook.com)

Arthur Johnson Evans

A Primer of Free Church History

A Primer of Free Church History . .

By A. JOHNSON EVANS, M.A.

1899

LONDON

H. R. ALLENSON

30 PATERNOSTER ROW, E.C.

PREFACE.

This little book has been written mainly with the object of interesting the young people of all ages who are connected with the Evangelical Free Churches, and of setting them on the right course of study in order to arrive at a proper knowledge of the history of their spiritual forefathers. For this purpose, great care has been taken to make the story historically accurate, or as nearly so as is possible within the limits assigned. The author has attempted to be strictly fair to men of all parties, and has avoided all assumptions that, in the conflicts of past times, one side was right and the other necessarily wrong. This method of writing, of course, deprives the reader of some of that glow which comes from the perusal of books that are more "partisan," but the loss is surely compensated by the increased historical sense which results from a more sober view of old controversies.

To those of us who are modestly, yet firmly, assured that we are holding to the highest truth that is possible for ourselves, there is no gain in refusing to grant that others may be right for themselves, though unable to agree with us on matters which, after all, transcend the powers of human finity.

The author may as well confess, once for all, that the treatment of the subject is unequal. Much more

Preface.

space has been given to the older "Dissenting" bodies than to those which originated in the eighteenth and nineteenth centuries. This was necessary to the purpose of the book, which aims at illustrating and elucidating, by historical narrative, our present position. But he wishes to guard against a misunderstanding which might arise among Baptist friends. He therefore would take this opportunity of saying (what will be found in the text), that as Baptist Churches are Congregational in their forms of government, and as the main interest of seventeenth century controversy was concerned with such questions, the word "Congregational" must please be taken as including both "Congregational" Churches, commonly so-called, and those who, because of the dogma which still to a certain extent divides them from their brethren have come to be called, by themselves and others, Baptists.

There will be found at the end of the book a short Bibliography. That list reveals the fact that there is a great need for much scientific work on this subject. Many of the defects of this Primer must be attributed to the lack of good standard histories of the various denominations. But, above all, the author looks forward to the advent of a sound history of the Free Churches as a whole, written by a scholar imbued with the modern historical spirit, yet enthusiastic enough to present to the world the inner meaning of British Nonconformity. If this Primer can do anything towards this consummation, the hopes of its author will be fully satisfied.

CONTENTS.

I

The Catholic Church and the Reformation   PAGE 1

    Introductory. Church Jurisdiction, (*a*) Voluntary, (*b*) Compulsory. Development of the "Holy Catholic Church." Demoralisation in the Catholic Church. National Reformation. The English Church. Origin of Congregational Churches. Their Difference from other Systems. Queen Elizabeth. Origin of Puritanism. The Elizabethan Church.

II

Separatism and Puritanism   20

    Fitz's Church and its Principles. Its Revolutionary Character. "Congregationalist" and Baptist. Separatist Pamphlets. Free Church Martyrs. English Presbyterians.

III

Separatists in Holland and America... ...   30

    Scrooby and Gainsborough. The Exiles in Holland. Differences among them. Increasing Difficulties. Emigration to New Plymouth. Religious Liberty (*a*) early, (*b*) lost, (*c*) rediscovered. The Baptist and the Congregationalist views.

Contents.

IV

The New England Way 47

Arminianism and Episcopacy by Divine Right, (a) enforced as the Truth, (b) opposed. The Book of the Prophet Mather. A Congregational Theocracy, (a) a Cambridge movement, (b) anti-sacerdotal, thorough, intolerant to outsiders. Its internal organisation. Public Worship. Its external organisation. Rhode Island and Maryland.

V

The Political Period of Presbyterianism and Congregationalism 63

Puritan Revolt. "Sectarian" activity. The "Dissenting Brethren" and their supporters. The Army, (a) Presbyterian, (b) "Sectarian." Toleration Controversy. Presbyterian v. Congregational. Oliver Cromwell. The Nominated Parliament. Cromwell's State-Church, (a) Creeds, (b) Appointments, (c) Illustrations. Baptists and Quakers. Stuart Restoration. The System of Spoils and the "Clarendon Code." New England till 1783. Pilgrim's Progress and Paradise Lost.

VI

The Sub-political Period 94

The "Presbyterian or Independent Denomination." Struggle between Catholic and Protestant. Declarations of Indulgence and the Toleration Act. Tory and Whig.

Contents.

VII
Religious Decadence 99
    Semi-parasitism. Indifference. Arianism and Deism. Decay of Discipline.

VIII
The Evangelical Revival 106
    Wesley and the effects of his teaching. Evangelicalism. The Modern State: National not Theocratic. Religious Liberty and Equality.

IX
The Catholic Revival 113
    Tractarianism. Nonconformist Churches.

X
The Present Day 118
    British Industry and the British Empire. The Churches in Arrear. Missionary Societies. New Denominations. Federation and Expansion. Religion in Elementary Schools. High Church v. Low Church. Disestablishment. Sacerdotalism. Conclusion.

Bibliography, A Brief 141

Chapter I.

The Catholic Church and the "Reformation."

Introductory.

Everyone knows that in England there are different sects of Christian people. Besides the Established Church which is represented in every parish, there are many kinds of Dissenters: Wesleyan and other Methodists, Baptists, Congregationalists, Quakers, Unitarians, Roman Catholics, and others. Some of these are older than others. Congregationalists, Baptists, and Presbyterians date from the 16th century, when Western Christendom began to be openly divided into many sections. The Society of Friends is one of many bodies which arose here in the 17th century, almost the only one of them which has survived. Nearly all the others, Wes-

A Primer of Free Church History.

leyan and other Methodists, Unitarians, Bible Christians, &c., are the results of 18th and 19th century movements.

The object of this primer is to attempt in short compass a historical explanation of the existence of these various bodies, specially of the older among them. Their conflicts in the 17th century are generally unknown or misunderstood, and yet a knowledge of them is necessary to a proper estimate, not only of our past, but of our present conflicts and agreements.

Christian people differ generally on questions of three kinds, viz.: doctrine or creed, forms of worship, forms of government or methods of managing their church affairs. These differences have arisen in the course of history and it is only by tracing, in however elementary a way, the development of events in the past that we can understand the reasons for these distinctions.

Church Jurisdiction.
(a) Voluntary.

From the Acts of the Apostles, the epistles of the New Testament and other sources, we know that the first preachers

The Catholic Church & the "Reformation."

of the Gospel formed their converts into churches which were quite independent one of another, though they were of course bound together in the unity of faith and love and had much mutual communication. These early churches had various kinds of officers, in imitation partly of the Jewish synagogues, partly of Greek and Roman institutions. The "bishops" and "deacons" had special charge of the poor, while the "presbyters" watched over the morals of the community. We may gather from such texts as Matt. xviii. 15-17 and 1 Cor. vi. 1, that each church exercised over its members both civil and criminal jurisdiction. Disputes were settled, and breaches of the moral law were punished without resort to the tribunals of the Roman Empire. Of course all this authority was exercised over willing subjects. The churches had no severer penalty than excommunication or expulsion from the body, but as the churches increased in number and in-

A Primer of Free Church History.

fluence, the penalties which they inflicted became socially more effective. When after 300 years the Roman Emperors were Christian, and the Empire began to support the Christian churches instead of persecuting them, this jurisdiction was made compulsory.

**Church Jurisdiction.
(b) Compulsory.**
When the Roman Empire had thus united with the Christian churches, a new conception began to grow among men. They believed that this triumph of the Christian church as a whole was the coming of the Kingdom of God. All men were compelled into its membership. To be a Roman and to be a Christian were one and the same thing. The Church governed the world. When in the fifth and following centuries the Roman power passed away before the inroad of "barbarians" from Germany, the Church survived the revolution, received the newcomers into its fold, converted them to its faith, and still contiued to exercise jurisdiction over them as of old. Until the "Reformation"

The Catholic Church & the "Reformation."

of the sixteenth century, whatever might happen in the rise and fall of kingdoms, all inhabitants of Western Europe felt themselves consciously to be parts of a world-wide power, the Christian Church. This power, as much as any modern State, had its laws, its officers, its courts, which were obeyed as much as, often more than, the commands of lay sovereigns. Kings and nobles were its protectors and its subjects. It was in a very real sense to the men of those times the Kingdom of God, ruling on earth through his divinely appointed representatives, the clergy of various ranks.

We must therefore conceive the Christian Church in the "middle ages" as a State, a government of men; different from other States, of course, with higher sanctions, holier aims, but yet subject to the laws of growth and development which we find in other governments. *[Development of the "Holy Catholic Church."]*

Very early there had begun to be a

difference acknowledged between "clergy" and "laity." In the necessary laxity of morals, a higher standard of purity was expected from the officials. The laity lost the powers of election which they had at first possessed, and the "presbyters" or "priests" as they came to be called, monopolised power. Bishops, in the course of theological disputes, came to be regarded as the guardians and definers of the "true faith," and gradually extended their authority over the priests. And lastly, because the bishops of Rome were placed in a peculiarly advantageous position and also because at various periods they took the lead in movements for reform and advance, they rose to a position of primacy in the West of Europe, and at last came to be regarded as the Heads of the "Catholic," i.e., Universal Church, under the name of "Popes."

Demoralisation in the Catholic Church But in the course of centuries, the Catholic Church, in spite of many attempts at reform, some of which

The Catholic Church & the "Reformation."

achieved more or less of success, gradually lost its spiritual life. The popes strove to gain for themselves territory in Italy. Bishops, richly endowed with land and political power neglected their duties, parish priests ceased to care for the character of their flocks. Monks and friars, whose orders had originally been founded from the best of motives by holy men to meet the evils of their times had become wealthy and attracted to their monasteries men of low ideals. Above all, the "ancient godly discipline" was lost. At first, when a man sinned, he had been excommunicated, and when he repented and was absolved from his excommunication, he was expected to submit to some punishment in proportion to the offence. Gradually, the necessity for true repentance was lost sight of, the idea of punishment for sin was materialised, the penance was regarded as balancing the sin and as somehow satisfying God's justice. Then came the more terrible abuses of Indulgences, until at last all earnest-minded men were anxious for reform, though they saw too clearly the difficulties in the way The Church had become so great a piece of machinery that a radical reform seemed almost impossible

National Reformation. It was when the Church was in this condition that Martin Luther began preaching in Germany. The result of his action and of other influences was a disruption of Christendom. Henceforward, instead of a reformation of the Universal Church, men aimed at reforming only that part of the Church which existed in their own country. Each kingdom, republic, or principality went its own way. In creed, some were Lutheran, some Calvinist, some Roman Catholic, but the unity of Christendom was lost. In the countries of the Continent which became Protestant, bishoprics disappeared; all the priests or ministers were regarded as equal. But the reformation in each case was national, and under the leadership of

The Catholic Church & the "Reformation."

princes or nobles they formed synods, which governed the country in each case as a whole. All the population was still subject to the clerical authorities, and the system was developed which has been called "presbyterianism" in contrast to the "episcopacy" which had preceded it. They thus made two steps towards primitive Christianity by rejecting the papacy and abolishing the bishoprics. This was the story of the Lutheran Churches of Germany, and of the Calvinistic Churches of the Netherlands, France, and Geneva.

But the story in England is different from all these. The monarchs of the Tudor family, Henry VIII. and his children, initiated the early stages of our Protestant history. Henry VIII., in 1529-36, destroyed the powers which the Pope had till then possessed in England, but made no further change in the government of the Church except to bring its whole machinery intact under the control of the Crown.

The English Church.

A Primer of Free Church History.

The advisers of his son, Edward VI.. (1547-53), pushed forward other changes, and the Church of England might have become Presbyterian if he had not died too soon for the revolution to be carried very far. After the brief period of reaction under Mary (1553-8), Elizabeth succeeded. She wished to follow in the footsteps of her father, and therefore retained the bishoprics; but she was necessarily anti-Papal and she inaugurated the Prayer Book of the Established Church, almost in the form in which it exists to-day.

Origin of Congregational Churches. But neither the "reformed" Churches of the Continent, whether Lutheran or Calvinist, nor the newly-independent English Church satisfied the desires of some Englishmen. They saw that while churches were national, while they acknowledged in their fold men of all kinds, the Church could never be thoroughly purified; and during Elizabeth's reign, these more ardent reformers began to appear here and there,

The Catholic Church & the "Reformation."

forming Churches of voluntary members. When they became conscious of their actions, and were noticed by others, this system of Church organisation gained for itself two names. Its advocates began to speak of it as the "Congregational" way, because they believed that each Church thus formed of true believers only, voluntarily joined together in a "particular congregation," had full rights of self-government. Those who opposed them, struck with their apparent exclusiveness of outward influence, nicknamed them "Independent."

We see therefore that we have to deal with three forms of church government, or attempts at enforcing discipline and maintaining the purity of the Church: Episcopal, Presbyterian, and Congregational. The first two divide Christendom territorially into provinces, dioceses, and parishes. These, the Episcopalians would govern by archbishops, bishops, and priests. The

Their Difference from other Systems.

A Primer of Free Church History.

Presbyterians would govern them by assemblies, classes, and kirk sessions. The Congregational way differs from them both. It regards Christendom not as a territory including all the inhabitants thereof, but as a collection of true believers scattered through the world among unbelievers, and divides them not territorially, but personally, allowing everyone liberty to join whatever Church he pleases, and leaving to every such Church full self-government as under the rule only of the one Divine Head of the Church Universal.

Queen Elizabeth. Elizabeth was Queen of England from 1558 to 1603, and, like all her house, has been called a despot, an epithet which may be retained if we realise rightly what is meant by it. She governed for the most part without Parliaments (the total of their sittings amounts to three years in the whole of her reign). She was supreme Governor of the Church of England, and made that governance a reality by means of

The Catholic Church & the "Reformation."

the statutory Court of High Commission and her strong objection to all discussion of Church matters in the House of Commons. But the most absolute despot has limits beyond which he may not pass. He cannot, without a mercenary army (and no Tudor was ever rich enough to maintain such a luxury), override the public opinion of his subjects in any matter on which they feel keenly. At the beginning of Elizabeth's reign, one half of the population was still of the old faith, and it would have been impossible for the Queen, even if she had been a thorough Puritan, to have pushed forward the Reformation faster than she could have taken with her the mass of her people. The reigns of Edward VI. and Mary, carefully studied, will teach us the truth of this maxim. There are two courses which might be considered possible for Elizabeth: she might on the one hand have risked her throne in the endeavour to bring all Englishmen up to the level of the most advanced, but it would have been a great risk to run. As it was, she only just saved herself and her country from ruin. Or we might suggest that she should at least have left everyone free to work out his salvation in the way that he thought right, giving complete liberty of action to all in Church matters. But this course would have been more difficult for Elizabeth than the former. Nay, on consideration, we may say it was a moral impossibility. We shall have reason to see, in the sequel of our story, how slowly the idea of religious liberty struggled into recognition, even among the most advanced thinkers. It would have been nothing short of a miracle for a sixteenth century prince to have conceived the thought. Most of the reformers themselves would have bitterly opposed the attempt to carry it into practice.

All that had been gained on the Continent had been liberty for each prince

The Catholic Church & the "Reformation."

or republic to choose the religion for their own district in each case. Nowhere had individuals gained the right to hold opinions differing from those of the rulers of their respective countries. It is even doubtful if any had claimed such a right. Minorities, where they existed, struggled, not for freedom, but for mastery. Christendom in the sixteenth century was in the same stage as Israel in the time of Elijah; when Jehovah had triumphed, "Take the prophets of Baal, and slay them with the sword." So was it also in England.

The Reformation, therefore, so it was thought, must be national. There must be one law for all, the more advanced must submit to wait till the least enlightened were prepared to keep step, and unity must be preserved so as to present an undivided front to the enemy who would have deposed Elizabeth, set Mary Stuart on the throne, and relighted the fires of Smithfield to restore the Papal supremacy.

A Primer of Free Church History.

To effect this unity, all men at that time, especially those in authority, thought that uniformity was necessary. The Lord is able to look on the heart, finite man can only judge by outward appearance, and Europe had as yet not learned the lesson, which we think we know by heart to-day, that outward uniformity is not always and everywhere necessary to inward unity of purpose.

Now all this may be granted without in any degree diminishing our respect and veneration for those who opposed the system established on such ideas. Nay, the more fully we realise the position of Elizabethan statesmen and the more freely we grant the common sense of their methods, so the more uncommon must we think the men who defied the system, the more thoroughly can we estimate and admire the clearness of their vision, the courage of their fidelity to a higher truth.

Origin of Puritanism. In the Established Church under Elizabeth, there were representd two schools of thought. One would make as few changes as possible and wished to retain as many of the old forms of worship as were compatible with the Calvinistic faith which all then equally held. The other wished to rid the Church of all such forms and ceremonies as would tend to draw ordinary folk back to the "superstitions" of which the nation had been purged. It is interesting to watch in the "Zürich letters" —a correspondence of the utmost value and interest which some Englishmen maintained with those who had been kind to them in exile—the gradual parting of the ways. Those who received bishoprics from Elizabeth step by step took the official view, that, though the ceremonies in dispute were in themselves indifferent, yet unity was all-desirable in the presence of so many dangerous enemies to the newly-independent Church and that unity was attainable only by the enforcement of uniformity. Those who did not accept offices began to argue that as the ceremonies were confessedly indifferent, a moderate degree of variety should be allowed. Thus arose in the Established Church two parties, "Puritan" and "Anti-Puritan." Both agreed in desiring that the reform, whether conservative or radical, should be national, i.e., that the whole nation should advance or stand still together.

The Elizabethan Church. Thus were laid down the lines on which the history of the Established Church of England has since journeyed swaying sometimes towards Rome, sometimes towards Geneva. Except during the period of the Puritan Revolution, whose story we shall tell, it has always retained the use of a written liturgy and the Episcopal form of government which is as old as the English Church itself. According to this system, England is divided into two provinces, governed respectively by the Archbishops of Canterbury and York. Under these are the bishops, governing

The Catholic Church & the "Reformation."

dioceses, and the priests who govern parishes. The country is divided territorially, and the assumption is that all the inhabitants of parish, diocese, or province are spiritual subjects of the clerical authorities. The whole system is bound together, and its working modified by the Supremacy of the Crown. The Queen is, at least so far as the Established Church is concerned, "over all persons and in all causes, within her dominions, supreme."

It was in opposition to this system, as an attempt made by Queen Elizabeth and her ministers to effect a reformation of manners and "to restore the ancient godly discipline" of the Church, that Congregational churches began to be formed.

Chapter II.

SEPARATISM AND PURITANISM.

Fitz's Church and its Principles.

Whether Lollards or other "heretics" before or during Henry VIII.'s time had any definite organisation has not yet been discovered. We know nothing of them but what can be gleaned from the records of their capture and condemnation. But the first Congregational Church in England of which we can definitely speak had already been founded when Elizabeth came to the throne. Its members resided in or near London, and they had for pastor a Mr. Fitz. We know, therefore, that from the very beginning of her reign, some Englishmen, how many it is impossible to say, had been acting on the principles which their spiritual descendants substantially hold to-day. They saw that the attempt at a national reformation which was being made by the Queen's government was by no means bringing the Church to the condition of primitive

Separatism and Puritanism.

times. When they went to the Lord's Supper in the "parish assemblies," they found themselves united therein with persons of various moral conditions, and they believed that they were committing sin by remaining in communion with such people. They believed it to be their duty to obey St. Paul's words to the Corinthians (2 Cor. vi. 17): "Come ye out from among them and be ye separate," especially as they saw no probability of the national reformation progressing any further in their time. If Elizabeth and her ministers could not restore the "ancient godly discipline" because there were, as was said at the time, men too great to submit, another way must be sought This way they found in the imitation of the Apostolic Churches, separating themselves from the world with which they were surrounded, at least in spiritual matters, and simply forming Churches consisting of those who were willing to join. Starting thus afresh, they turned to the New Testament again for directions, and imitated the offices and organisation of Corinthian and other Churches. They provided themselves with pastors, teachers, elders, widows, &c., assuming that what form of Church government was discoverable in the New Testament had been expressly ordained by Jesus Christ for all time. They claimed an exclusive Divine Sanction for Congregationalism.

Its Revolutionary Character But this method of reformation—by private effort instead of using State machinery, working from below upward, from within outward, as distinct from the method of affecting the personal life by ceremonies imposed by authority—this method which appears so simple to us who are accustomed to the development of Free Churches, was in the sixteenth century regarded as a revolution, scarcely to be comprehended, and, in so far as it was understood, dangerous. It was unique, unprecedented in the memory of Christen-

Separatism and Puritanism.

dom, a memory which had been so filled with the Mediæval conception of a Universal Church, a Kingdom of God which had included men of all sorts, that it had forgotten the first three hundred years of Christian story, when the church had no relation with the State except through occasional persecution.

Each Congregational church was independent of others. They might conceivably differ to any possible amount on every article of faith. But on the whole they agreed in theological matters with one another, and, as yet, with the Established Church from which they had separated. There was, however, one point on which a difference existed, which then, and till now, has separated churches agreeing in almost all other points, and especially in their views on church government. Some thought that children of believers should be baptised in infancy as typifying the belief that they were "within

"Congregationalist" and Baptist.

A Primer of Free Church History.

the covenant." Others as firmly believed that no one should be baptised unless they had individually arrived at such a condition of heart and mind that they were fit to be received as full members of a Christian church. They also thought that baptism should be by immersion, as was the custom of the early churches and the rule of the Catholic Church. This is still the one point of difference between those who have been called Congregationalists and those who, though not differing from the others in matters of church government, have been called Baptists. What, therefore, is said in this primer on Congregationalism applies equally to "Congregational" and to "Baptist" churches, unless it is expressly stated otherwise.

Separatist Pamphlets. After twenty years of existence, the Congregationalists began to express their principles in printed pamphlets. Robert Browne, a nephew of Lord Burleigh, was their first spokesman; in

Separatism and Puritanism.

1580 he published a tract with the title, "Of Reformation without Tarrying for any." But more famous than this was a series of satirical papers that appeared during the four or five years succeeding the defeat of the Spanish Armada, over the signature of "Martin Marprelate." They were of course printed secretly, and the Government never quite succeeded in their attempts to discover the author or authors of them. Their style is difficult for us properly to appreciate or even thoroughly to understand, but beneath the bitterness of theological strife and the personal scurrility which was then rarely absent from controversy we perceive the principles of the writers clearly displayed.

They were willing to acknowledge the Queen's authority in all temporal matters, while strenuously denying her right to any special position in the Church. On Congregational principles no one may occupy any position but that of an ordinary member of a particular

A Primer of Free Church History.

Church, unless he is chosen by such a Church to office in the body. But this contention, which flows naturally from the Congregational position, was, in the eyes of Elizabeth's advisers, dangerously like the claim of the Roman Catholics. They also disclaimed the Queen's Spiritual Supremacy, only to demand it for the Italian bishop whose "foreign jurisdiction" most Englishmen were striving to keep out of the realm.

Free Church Martyrs. It is from this double point of view that controversies have arisen regarding the nature of the punishment inflicted on those who published the "Martin Marprelate" and similar tracts. While the advocates of the bishops argue that the pamphlets were "seditious," the friends of the martyrs deny, with perfect truth, the allegation that they were hostile to the Queen's Government.

In 1593, three Congregationalists were hanged in London for having

Separatism and Puritanism.

spread this literature. Their fame is, or ought to be, in all the Churches. John Penry, the enthusiastic young Welshman whose heart's desire was the conversion of his native country from the "darkness" of Roman Catholicism, was generally believed at the time to be the original "Martin Marprelate." John Greenwood was, as far as we know, Puritan from his youth up, and Henry Barrowe was a converted courtier, whom Dr. Dexter believes to have been the real author of the "Marprelate" tracts. They were all graduates of the Universities, Greenwood and Barrowe of Cambridge, and Penry of Oxford.

We have been able to tell the story of these Congregationalists more fully, because six years ago, much attention was drawn to the matter. Baptists had more martyrs than their brethren in separation, but their number is so great and the records of their opinions are so disputed and doubtful, that we must not enter upon the matter at length.

A Primer of Free Church History.

English Presbyterians.

Before Robert Browne had formulated the principles of Congregationalism, Scotland in so far as it was Protestant, had gone far towards the abolition of bishops. Some English Puritans, that is, members of the Established Church who wished for more reform than Elizabeth's Government would approve but who did not go so far as to separate from the Established Church, had begun to advocate the same in England. The government which they discovered in the New Testament and for which they claimed an exclusive Divine Sanction was similar to that of the "reformed" Churches of the Continent. Dr. Cartwright (Lady Margaret Professor of Divinity at Cambridge) had formulated the theory in his academical lectures, and some clergymen in Surrey had proceeded, while retaining their offices in the Established Church, to form a presbytery, i.e., to unite to form a government of their district by "teaching" and "ruling" elders. Thus

Separatism and Puritanism.

began to appear in England, Presbyterianism, an organisation of the whole area of England in which the diocese was to be governed by an assembly instead of a bishop, smaller districts by "classes" instead of an archdeacon, and parishes by "kirk-sessions" instead of the one parson. But they considered, as did their Episcopal opponents, that every inhabitant of parish, district, or diocese was to be subject to the ecclesiastical authorities, just as he was subject to the lay authorities. The Church was still to consist of men of all sorts. It was only another way of enforcing discipline on those who were unwilling as well as those who were willing members of the Christian Church. Much of British history in the seventeenth century consists of the conflict between these two systems, Episcopacy and Presbyterianism. In the end, neither of them succeeded in producing a pure Church, neither re-established the much desired "godly discipline."

Chapter III.

Separatists in Holland and America.

Scrooby and Gainsborough.

The Mohammedans date their years from that event in the prophet's life which is called in the Arab speech the Hejra, or flight from Mecca to Medina in the year 622. We also have a flight to record in the annals of the Free Churches whose consequences have been momentous in world-history, and which is told for us in Dr. Brown's "Pilgrim Fathers" in a way that thrills us as we read the simple but eloquent story. Time would fail us to tell of the heroes known and unknown, of the great spiritual struggles which have made the names of Scrooby, Austerfield, and Gainsborough for ever famous: of William Brewster, William Bradford, John Clyfton, John Smyth, and, above all, of John Robinson, men who resigned their homes and positions in England and went out with their families, not knowing whither, so that they

Separatists in Holland and America.

might maintain the purity of the Christian Church and the progress towards a completer reformation which was being hindered, as they believed, by a reaction among the rulers of the National Church towards the end of Elizabeth's and in the beginning of James I.'s reign.

The Exiles in Holland. Imprisoned for continuing in England to carry out their conception of a pure Church and to simplify their forms of worship, imprisoned for attempting to escape, many of them were finally allowed in 1609 to find a refuge in the cities of Holland. These English clergymen and the husbandmen who formed their congregations, stripped of almost all their possessions, went to a land of foreign speech and foreign ways, in order that they might maintain the worship of God and the Church discipline which were dearer to them than life itself. They were compelled to seek a livelihood in the narrow streets of Amsterdam, Leyden, and other cities of the Netherlands, and the modern traveller who would trace their footsteps must seek the sites of their places of worship and abode among the slums of those busy commercial cities.

Differences among them. But here at least they were free from outside persecution. The conditions were hard and they never seem to have done more than earn a bare subsistence, but their church-life had full scope. Now it is important constantly to remember that these were exiles for conscience' sake, men and women who held the Truth to be the one object of life to seek, and when found to hold fast. No consideration would hinder them from following out in action the convictions of their souls, and the fact that they were picked men, chosen by what we have learned to call the "survival of the fittest," will prepare us to find all of them independent thinkers, untramelled by any consideration for fellowmen. Much, therefore, of the story of the Separatist

Separatists in Holland and America.

exiles consists of controversies and we find them diverging one from another in the working out of the problem of church constitutions. Dr. Dexter distinguishes four different schools of thought amongst them. Robert Browne had argued that the Government of each church should be conducted in all its details by the members, all being equal. Barrowe had wished to make the government of the churches less democratic and to give more power to the officers. In this tendency there were different degrees. For example, Francis Johnson, the " pastor " of the Church in Amsterdam, would have the power confined entirely to the "elders," while Ainsworth, the "teacher" of the same church, wished it to be shared with the unofficial members. John Robinson agreed with Ainsworth in this contention, but was broader-minded than others in a point that was greatly discussed among the exiles. They had, as we have seen, regarded the Episcopalian

A Primer of Free Church History.

Church and its members as anti-Christian, and therefore not to be communicated with. Robinson, however, argued that there was no need to assume such an extreme position, and always recognised the "parish assemblies" in England as "true churches," communicating freely with their members.

Increasing Difficulties. In much suffering and in narrowed ways of life, with many differences both amongst themselves and with the Dutch Presbyterian churches by which they were surrounded, yet tolerated by the rulers and sometimes welcomed by their universities (indeed, Robinson made himself famous in their theological disputes), the exiles lived in the Netherlands for eleven years (1609-20) of the truce between Holland and Spain. But in 1620, the sky of Europe was dark with the clouds of war. The Protestant nobles of Bohemia had rejected their Jesuit king, and had chosen Frederick, the Elector Palatine, in his stead. He had been driven out of Bohemia in the

Separatists in Holland and America.

spring of 1620, and Protestants and Roman Catholics were arming in Germany for what proved to be a thirty years' war. The truce between the King of Spain and his long rebellious subjects of the Netherlands had ended, and as he was not yet willing to recognise their independence, the war was on the eve of breaking out again. Some members, therefore, of Robinson's church at Leyden began to bethink themselves of their position. It had long before been said mockingly to them, "Why don't you take yourselves off to America?" and now that the dangers of war were probably to be added to their other distresses, they began seriously to consider the problem.

Many considerations tended to induce them to emigrate. They saw their children growing up under influences which they regarded as harmful. Their Dutch neighbours did not keep the Sabbath with the strictness of the English Separatists, regarding their

A Primer of Free Church History.

Puritan ideas of the day, indeed as an "English fiction." The young men, weary of the laborious toil, were enlisting for the wars and were thus being lost to the Church; at least, they would naturally grow up as Dutchmen, intermarry with their neighbours, and be lost to England. The exiles had no desire to cast off their allegiance to the English crown, and if they could settle in some yet vacant lands within the dominions of King James (1603-25), where they could at the same time extend the power of their native country and have liberty to carry out their ideas of church discipline, they would be willing to venture much. Besides, they would be glad to return to their agricultural pursuits, and they thought it possible to do something for the Indians of North America. It is easily seen that these men were broad-minded, occupied with thoughts that are now called Imperialist and Catholic.

Separatists in Holland and America.

They had two difficulties—want of money, and the need to avoid exciting the suspicion of the English authorities. Accordingly they had to go out under the auspices—financed by them, as we should say—of a trading company in London. They went across to Southampton in the "Speedwell," and thence with others in the "Speedwell" and "Mayflower." Many were their difficulties even on the voyage. The "Speedwell" either broke down or was represented by its master as unseaworthy, and when the "Mayflower" at last reached the coast of America, winter was coming on.

Emigration to New Plymouth.

Of some of their difficulties we may read in Longfellow's beautiful poem, "The Courtship of Miles Standish"; but the sufferings of that winter were no poetry, they were grim reality, and only half the emigrants survived to see the spring. But these men and women of steel did not go back, like those who had made previous attempts at coloni-

A Primer of Free Church History.

sation, and they remained to plant on the shores of the New World what has been as yet found impossible in the Old, a State in which laws on the subject of religion were unknown.

Religious Liberty. "A State in which laws on the subject of religion were unknown"—to understand the significance of this phrase we must look backwards for a time. The first three centuries of Christian history have presented us with the view of a Church which had no relations with the State except that of occasional persecutions. The Pagan Roman Empire neither patronised nor controlled the actions of Christians as such, never interfered with the internal action of the churches. But, with the accession of Constantine in 323, the State and Church began to enter into friendly relations and before long there was a complete union between them. This difference of situation brought about a change in the opinions of Christians as to the duty of governors. We

Separatists in Holland and America.

see it most clearly in the words of St. Augustine, Bishop of Hippo, who said, in a letter written at the end of the fourth century, "My opinion was at first that no one should be compelled to the unity of Christ, but drawn by words, met in discussion, convinced by reason, lest we should receive as pretended Catholics those whom we had known as open heretics. But this opinion of mine was overthrown not by the words of opponents but by the logic of facts. For at first my city was totally opposed to me and sided with the Donatist party, but has been turned to Catholic unity by fear of the Imperial laws, so that now this pernicious opinion is so detested that one might believe it had never existed."

For over a thousand years it was the universal opinion of Christendom that the duty of governments was to maintain the Truth by all means in their power. It was believed that thus could be established the Kingdom of God on

Religious Government.

A Primer of Free Church History.

earth. The "Reformation" of the sixteenth century made no change in this respect; rather was freedom of opinion narrowed by the multiplication of rival creeds. It was not till each sect of Christendom in turn had suffered from what they thus learned to call not "prosecution" but "persecution" that it began to dawn on the minds of more than a few speculative thinkers—and these only in their speculations, not their practical life—that any other course was conceivable, much less to be approved of as right. Naturally Episcopalians and Presbyterians who still believed that Christendom should be governed on the territorial basis, did not discover the new-old principle, nor did they welcome it when it first appeared.

Religious Liberty Again. We should, however, expect that Congregationalists would naturally arrive at the principle of religious liberty—of complete severance of Church and State. The principle is

Separatists in Holland and America.

logically inherent in the Congregational way. If churches are to be built up by the voluntary union of individuals, and if such churches are to be completely self-governed, there is evidently no room in such a system for the action of the Prince as such. But so illogical is human nature, so apt are we to solve only the practical problem while ignoring or rejecting "mere theories," that it was not the pædobaptist (infant-baptising) Congregationalists who were the first advocates of "religious liberty," but the Baptists.

Herein, indeed, we find in the 17th century a further point of difference between the two groups of churches. The body which is most persecuted, most evil spoken of will be that which first evolves the principle of "liberty" in and for itself. Now, consider the basis of Baptist principles. Instead of registering their children as members of the Catholic Church, the Baptists, or as they were called in the 17th century,

The Baptist View.

A Primer of Free Church History.

Anabaptists, left the admission till they were of age to decide for themselves, and then made it a matter of free choice for the individual to join or to refrain. The Catholic Church was a State; the National Churches which had arisen at the Reformation were but the ecclesiastical aspect of the various States. Imagine the modern parallel therefore to the action of 17th century Baptists. Suppose it were now claimed that children should not be expected to obey the laws of a country till they were old enough to choose, and then were free to obey or not, according to their free judgment. We should call such a state of things Anarchy. So did 17th century folk regard the Baptist principle and practice. Such rebellion on principle was naturally "persecuted," and peaceable Baptists suffered also because they were generally supposed to sympathise with that mysterious movement in the German city of Münster, where, in the 16th century, some ad-

Separatists in Holland and America.

vanced thinkers had prematurely endeavoured to set up a "Kingdom of God," and had thus, actively or passively, given occasion for scenes of great disorder. Persecuted thus by all parties the Baptists may be expected to be the first to evolve the doctrine of religious liberty, and we are not surprised when we come across the following story:—
John Smyth, the "Se-Baptist," of Amsterdam, died in 1611, leaving his exiled English flock in the charge of Helwisse. They drew up a covenant in which, among other statements of principle, they say: "The magistrate, by virtue of his office, is not to meddle with religion or matters of conscience, nor compel men to this or that form of religion or doctrine, but to leave the Christian religion to the free conscience of everyone . . . because Christ alone is the King and Lawgiver of the Church and Conscience."

But the Pædobaptist Congregationalists did not advance so far as this. They *The Congregationalist View.*

did not yet advocate toleration as a principle. They looked rather to such texts as Isa. xlix. 23, 1 Tim. ii. 2, and Rev. xvii. 16, and even John Robinson, of Leyden, whose catholicity of thought we have already mentioned, said in express answer to the Baptists of Amsterdam :

"This (James iv. 12) indeed proves that he (the magistrate) may alter, devise, or establish nothing in religion otherwise than Christ hath appointed, but proves not that he may not use his lawful power lawfully for the furtherance of Christ's Kingdom and laws," and this when so many were differing radically as to what "Christ's Kingdom and laws" really were. We therefore surmise that the reason for the covenant which the Pilgrim Fathers drew up on board the "Mayflower" when in sight of the New World, was that they differed among themselves as to the ideal of the Christian Church (Miles Standish has been supposed to have

Separatists in Holland and America.

been a Roman Catholic), and that this erection of a "civil body politic" was a necessary measure of mutual protection in their peculiar circumstances.*

> *"Ay, call it holy ground*
> *The soil where first they trode.*
> *They have left unstain'd what there they found,*
> *Freedom to worship God."*

They were willing to try the great experiment; but, if they were true disciples of the pastor whom they had left behind at Leyden and whom they were destined never to meet on earth again, they would have preferred, like all but a few in the seventeenth century, to have enforced the Truth. Unless we realise that they regarded this as their greatest virtue, we shall always misunderstand the founders of New Plymouth. Not liberty for all to

---
* See the "Seven Articles which the Church at Leyden sent to the Council of England, to be considered of in respect of their judgments occasioned about their going to Virginia," printed by Dr. Brown in "Pilgrim Fathers of New England," pp. 175-6.

A Primer of Free Church History.

wander into "error," but the maintenance, by all means, governmental or other, of the Truth as it is in Jesus, was the ideal of all but Baptists and Quakers when Stuarts were ruling in England.

Chapter IV.

THE NEW ENGLAND WAY.

Towards the end of Elizabeth's reign there had begun a reaction in the Established Church of England against the Calvinistic doctrines which almost all had till then shared and which had been embodied in "the 39 Articles" (1562-71). The doctrines advocated by Hermann, the Dutch theologian, and hence called Arminianism were spreading in England as elsewhere. Whereas Calvin had insisted on the equality of all men in the common condemnation by God from which only the predestined were to be saved, the Arminians argued that men differed from one another in moral deserts. The two doctrines are

Arminianism and Episcopacy by Divine Right,

A Primer of Free Church History.

placed side by side in Lord Tennyson's "In Memoriam":

"*For merit lives from man to man,
But not from man, O Lord, to Thee.*"

In the Arminian scheme of theology, more room was found for "works," and by those who followed this teaching in England these "works" came to include the various ministrations of the Church services, specially the "Holy Communion." Closely connected with these views, if not a logical result from them, were an exaltation of the clerical office and sacerdotal ideas. Whereas Englishmen had been accustomed to "ministers" presiding at the "table" of "communion," they now again began to see "priests" offering on an "altar," holy "sacrifices."

Further, whereas Richard Hooker, defending Episcopacy against Presbyterianism and Separatism, had argued in his "Ecclesiastical Polity" that, whatever form of church government

The New England Way.

might be discoverable in the New Testament, each generation was at liberty to adopt that form which best suited them, and had thus denied exclusive Divine Sanction to every kind of church organisation, now Bancroft and others followed the example of Cartwright and the Separatists, and claimed Apostolic sanction and everlasting obligation for their own Episcopalian system.

The great advocate of these various views was William Laud, who in the years 1620-40 was rising from bishopric to archbishopric, and with the help of Charles I. and their friend Sir Thomas Wentworth was enforcing the government in Church and State which they called, in their private correspondence, "Thorough." Archbishop Laud did not differ from others except in the scope of his views. He, too, like the Separatists, had large ideals for the British Isles and the "Catholic Church." His aim was a great Church-State, uniform in both lay and ecclesiastical

Enforced as the Truth;

A Primer of Free Church History.

matters, in which "men of light and leading" should rule, and his ideas on the "beauty of holiness" be carried out in worship and discipline. Not only in England was this rule to be enforced, but in Roman Catholic Ireland, among the colonists of South Virginia, and even among the exiles in the Netherlands and New England.

Opposed. But, while many sympathised with Laud's ideals, sympathies which are enshrined, for example, in the poetry of George Herbert, there were also many who opposed him bitterly, and who, more and more, as the years went by, emigrated to America. These fugitives from the ritualism of William Laud were the Puritans who founded the greater part of New England.

The Book of the Prophet Mather. Whoever would read at large of this great movement should find in some library (for it is not now to be bought) Cotton Mather's great folio, written in 1695, and published in 1702. As the compiler of the history of the Crusades

The New England Way.

called his collection "Gesta Dei per Francos" (That which God hath wrought by the Franks), so the seventeenth century New Englander entitled his work "Magnalia Christi Americana" (The Great Things of Christ in America). If ever the English race should realise the sacred character of their high calling, this work would assuredly form part of their Bible. The author says: "In some resemblance to the Israelites, in the settlement of New England, there were several instances wherein that army of confessors was under a theocracy; for their laws were still enacted, and their wars were still directed by the Voice of God, as far as they understood it, speaking from the oracle of the Scriptures: and though they elected their own judges, yet these were so provided by God that the Blessed people were still sensibly (i.e., evidently) governed by the Lord of all." He constantly describes the formation of new settlements with the phrases, 'a church was gathered,' 'became a church,' 'being in-churched.' We are reminded of the patriarchs who, here or there, "built an altar to the Lord."

A Congregational Theocracy;

These Puritans—Evangelical sons of the Church of England, whose extremest views at home had been to rid themselves of bishops and reduce Church government to the equality of "presbyters" as they saw it on the Continent— no sooner landed in America than they developed Congregationalism. Cotton Mather tells us they consulted their brethren at New Plymouth, but indeed, with their scattered settlements, it was not easily possible for them to be other than Congregational. Whenever a township was collected, they erected a "meeting house" for all public purposes whether civil or religious, they "gathered a church" and regarded the governing part of the community as consisting of the members thereof. For the founders of Massachusetts and Connecticut were in one respect, and that a

The New England Way.

supremely important one, different from the Pilgrim Fathers. They did not establish liberty, but a pure theocracy: to use Mather's words, "A powerful party (William Laud and his fellow-thinkers) resolving not only to separate (note the counter charge of separation) from the communion of all the faithful that were averse to certain confessedly unscriptural and uninstituted (i.e., not sanctioned by Jesus Christ) rites in the worship of God, but also to persecute with destroying severities those who were nonconformists (don't misunderstand this word) thereto, compelled a considerable number of good men to seek a shelter among the salvages of America." These exiles believed themselves to be the true Church of England from which the bishops had "separated." They were now driven into the wilderness, and they would maintain there the purity which had been impossible in the mother country. Circumstances forced them into Congregation-

A Primer of Free Church History.

alism, and they gave the franchise only to those who were full members of their respective churches. No one was compelled to this membership, but on the other hand no one was permitted to stay in the colony who attempted to set up any other form of church government. Thomas Dudley, a New England minister who died in 1653, wrote:—

"*Let Men of God in Courts and Churches watch*
O'er such as do a Toleration hatch,
Lest that ill egg bring forth a cockatrice
To poison all with heresie and vice."

(a) A Cambridge Movement. The New England Way, the furthest development of Congrgationalism in the seventeenth century, was so significant a product and had so great an influence on British history, that we must pause to give a more complete account of it. It was, pre-eminently, a University movement, and of the two English Universities, Cambridge had far the greater share. Of the colleges in Cambridge,

The New England Way.

Christ's and S. John's, the two foundations of Lady Margaret Beaufort, mother of Henry VII., had been destined to be nurseries of the new learning of her time, viz., the study of Greek. They had been in the forefront of the advancing tide of thought in the sixteenth century, and had only been surpassed in their zeal for Puritanism towards the end of Elizabeth's reign by the new college of Emmanuel, founded by the Puritan courtier, Sir Walter Mildmay. Harvard, who founded the first American college, was from Emmanuel, and it was not without reason that the Congregational theocracy of New England named their University town, Cambridge.

Opposed therefore to the Oxford or High Church movement of William Laud and his associates, was a Cambridge or Puritan movement, an activity which has had a continuous existence in England, and which had an immediate and lasting success in

America. In the two hundred and fifty years that have since elapsed, the movement has there followed the lines of a logical development and has expanded into what we see to-day on the unparalleled scale of the United States.

(b) Anti-Sacerdotal. The Puritan clergy, unable at first to hold their own in England, emigrated to the New World and, finding to their astonishment a field of unbounded expansion where they had expected to live in poverty and narrowness, they developed the Congregational plan. Their theology was Calvinist, and they were totally opposed to all sacerdotalism; with Rome and its system they held no relations but those of unmitigated hostility, and their opposition to the Laudian school of thought was best expressed when they regarded it as tending, if not leading directly, to "Popery."

Thorough. They were tenacious of ecclesiastical discipline. Members of Congregational churches watched over one another—in love, it is true—but there was a real

The New England Way.

mutual superintendence which extended to every department of life that could be regarded as moral or religious. No one might even move from the church of which he was a member (i.e., from the settlement of which he was a part) without the leave of the community, and it was thought unworthy that he should desire this merely with the view of bettering his worldly position. It need not be said that they were strict Sabbatarians, and in many other ways they derived their views from the Old Testament, e.g., on the question of witches and their treatment.

Quakers were, perhaps, their special abhorrence, because of their "irregular" ways and because of their preference of the "light within" to the "Written Word." Puritanism abhorred the "enthusiasms" of George Fox's followers. Yet it would be a mistake to imagine that there was uniformity of thought in New England. The more we know their story in detail, the more we rea- *Intolerant to Outsiders.*

lise that there was much difference of opinion, and much kindly tolerance of one another's peculiarities.

Its Internal Organisation. Having the "northern parts of Virginia" almost entirely to themselves, the New Englanders developed views on Church government both as to internal organisation and in their mutual relations. John Robinson of Leyden had exhorted his flock to avoid the "odious name of Brownists," and indeed all Congregationalists both in old England and in New constantly repudiated the epithet. It seems to have been used, like the word Anabaptist, as a term of reproach, and to have sounded in seventeenth century ears much the same as "anarchist" does in ours. Browne's principle—that all the male members had equal rights to take part in the direct government of the church—was disliked as "popular," and it was only the New Plymouth colonists who still continued to practise it. Other New England Congregationalists followed the

The New England Way.

principles of Barrowe and gave to the officers more authority; Eliot, the apostle to the Indians, "perceived in New England Congregationalism a sweet sort of temperament between rigid Presbyterianism and levelling Brownism, so that on the one side the liberties of the people are not oppressed and overlaid; on the other side, the authority of the elders is not rendered insignificant." Stone, a New England minister, put the matter epigrammatically when he described Congregationalism as "a speaking aristocracy in the face of a silent democracy."

New England principles in the matter of public worship may be summarised in Samuel Mather's paraphrase of the Second Commandment: "Thou shalt not make any graven image or form of worship to thyself": and they therefore confined themselves to extempore prayer, reading God's Word, and singing paraphrases of the Psalms. They paid so little heed to beauties of style that they wished to have a more literal rendering than that which they had brought from England. It was only their abhorrence of chanting which hindered their use of the "Authorised Version."

Partly because they required the whole of the six days to earn their living, partly because they tended to take the Fourth Commandment, as they did many other Biblical precepts, quite literally, all the church activities were confined to the Sabbath, which they regarded as beginning at Saturday sunset. Their services were not renowned for their brevity; besides worship and preaching, the work that is now carried on in separate church meetings was undertaken on the Sabbath, so that it was a busy day for them. Occasionally they had great days of intercession, when they would continue without a break from nine in the morning till five in the afternoon, prayers of an hour in length being alternated with sermons of

The New England Way.

an hour or two, the short intervals being filled with the singing of a psalm.

In the matter of mutual relations between churches, the New Englanders were in advance of Old English Congregationalism. Being practically unanimous in all essentials, they naturally tended to union, and "synods" were held to meet difficulties or to draw up a common Confession of Faith. They granted that synods had much power over particular churches, and they came to differ from Presbyterians only on one or two points, but these were important. Presbyterian synods had power to act directly on an individual Christian, even in opposition if necessary to the church of which he was a member. Congregationalists left the carrying out of synodal decisions to the particular church. If one church differed from the rest, Presbyterians excommunicated that church as a part of "discipline"—Congregationalists in the like instance "withdrew from communion" with that church.

External Organisation.

A Primer of Free Church History.

Rhode Island and Maryland. We must not pass away from our sketch of New England without a mention of Roger Williams, who arrived in 1631, and after five years of conflict with the authorities, was ejected from the colony because he persisted, in season and out of season, in his advocacy of "soul-liberty," the absolute right of every individual Christian to live only to his Master. It is impossible not to sympathise both with the large and tender-hearted hero of these impossible Utopias and with those who realised the necessity of some amount of government in order to defend the liberty which had been gained. Driven out of Massachusetts, he became the founder of Rhode Island, a colony which shares with New Plymouth and the Roman Catholic plantations of Maryland, the honour of being founded on the basis of absolute religious liberty for all.

Chapter V.

THE POLITICAL PERIOD OF PRESBYTERIANISM AND CONGREGATIONALISM. 1637-1677.

When, in 1637, Archbishop Laud followed up his success in re-establishing Episcopacy by Divine Right in Scotland with an attempt to introduce a Prayer-Book slightly more "Popish" than the Anglican, he brought home to every Lowlander the meaning of his movement. The result was an almost universal uprising, and the course of events which led to Civil War in the three kingdoms. Puritan England, organised in the Parliament, first swept away the system in Church and State which they detested, and then the majority of the Commons and the minority of the Lords entered on a conflict with the King on *Puritan Revolt.*

the field of battle. The last bill to which Charles I. was forced to give his assent was one for the removal of the bishops from the House of Lords, but the rebel part of the Parliament soon began to advance much further than this. They appointed a large committee of "Divines" (i.e., clergymen) to advise them on ecclesiastical matters, a body which was known as the Westminster assembly, and by 1644 Parliament and Assembly had superseded the Book of Common Prayer in favour of a "Directory of Public Worship" which prescribed services very like what is to-day usual in "old-fashioned" nonconformist churches, had sanctioned the "Longer" and the "Shorter Catechism," and had gone far in establishing Presbyterianism as the form of government for the Established church.

Sectarian Activity. But the majority of the "Long Parliament" and of the Westminster Assembly had not even begun to formulate their scheme of reform and to Presbyterianise

The Political Period 1637—1677.

the Church of England, when there appeared an opposition, not so much from the defeated and disheartened Episcopalians, as from the numerous "sects" which, in the conflict of authorities, began to abound. The exiles returned almost entirely from the Netherlands. The Baptists, who had previously returned because they thought it wrong to flee from persecution, and who had recently maintained their churches even in London during Laud's rule, began to appear openly, and New England began to take part in the politics of the mother country. Some few colonists returned to take part in the war and in controversy, and the Congregationalists on both sides of the Atlantic worked together for their common purposes so far as the distance and difficulty of communication would allow. Much was heard during those years of "the New England way," and the Congregationalists of Old England used the American constitutional developments

A Primer of Free Church History.

to urge a compromise with their "Presbyterian brethren."

The years of the Civil War and the Commonwealth (1640-60) may thus be regarded as the "political period" of Congregationalism, the period during which it aimed at and gained a commanding position in the politics of the country.

The "Dissenting Brethren" and their Supporters. The Congregational movement was evidently large and influential, and it was represented in the Westminster Assembly by certain "Divines" who, because of their persistent obstruction, came to be known as the "Five Dissenting Brethren." Besides the great body of opinion which supported them in Old and New England, they were helped by many in the Parliament who were neither Episcopalian or Presbyterian. Some of these were Erastians, who believed that no ecclesiastical power should be allowed in the country, but that the State, the lay power, should control all equally, and were therefore

The Political Period 1637—1677.

as much opposed to Presbyterianism by Divine Right, as to Episcopacy by the same sanction.

But, when men have once appealed to the sword, by the decision of the sword must they remain; and to realise the importance of each political party in the years 1642-53, we must look not to Assembly or Parliament, but to the army. Now the Parliament had at first raised an orthodox force, under the conduct of Manchester, Essex, and others, moderate Presbyterians, whose great anxiety was to preserve the ancient constitution of the kingdom, and who, while wishing to limit the power of the King, were of no mind to destroy either his person or his office, if he would consent to a thorough reformation in the Church. In 1643, in sore need of help, the English Parliament made a treaty with the Scots, the Solemn League and Covenant, whereby, in return for military help, the English promised to attempt a reformation of the Churches in

The Army.
(a) Presbyterian.

England and Ireland "according to the Word of God and the example of the best Reformed Churches," i.e., those of Geneva and the Netherlands. By this clause, the Scots always maintained that the English Parliament pledged themselves to establish Presbyterianism.

The Army; (b) "Sectarian." But the phrase, "the Word of God and" had been inserted in the treaty by one of the commissioners, Sir Harry Vane, a Congregationalist, with the express intention of extending the reference. In this action Vane was representing the feelings of the regiments that had been formed during the war, mainly in the Eastern Counties, by a gentleman farmer of Huntingdon, Oliver Cromwell.

In forming his troops of cavalry, Cromwell had felt the need of an inspiration for them, to oppose to the sense of honour and loyalty which were the motives of the best cavaliers. He therefore sought for men who "had the root of the matter in them." He acted

The Political Period 1637—1677.

on the principle that good soldiers must be made of good men, and that real heart-felt religion was the only foundation of moral goodness. Accordingly, Cromwell formed a cavalry force of "God-fearing" men. He was not particular as to their form of creed, so long as they had a belief in God as their Saviour from sin, and an earnest desire to live for His honour and glory. These men, soon to be known as "Ironsides," a nickname originally given to Cromwell himself, varying among themselves on religious questions, but in general neither Episcopalian nor Presbyterian, maintained the cause of the "Five Dissenting Brethren," and their sympathisers in Parliament and the country —a cause which was expressed in the demand they made for Toleration.

It is all-important to understand this word and its use in the seventeenth century. Those who advocated toleration were by no means of the same mind as John Smyth's followers, or Roger Wil- **The Toleration Controversy.**

liams. The Baptists would have followed the example of the Pilgrim Fathers and have established a "civil body politic" in which all forms of Christianity, even all forms of religion, would have been equal before the law. "Religious equality," as this ideal has been called, was, in the seventeenth century, only the peculiarity of the "most extreme." It was in general abhorred by all practical statesmen. What was demanded by the more "orthodox" of those who opposed intolerant Episcopacy and Presbyterianism, was not the disestablishment of the Church, but toleration for those who could not belong to whichever form of Church government and worship should be established. And even in this contention, there were endless shades of difference. Moderate Presbyterians—i.e., members of the Westminster Assembly and others who did not regard all toleration as the devil's device for the destruction of souls—would have been willing to allow

The Political Period 1637—1677.

toleration to their brethren, the orthodox Congregationalists, if these did not demand it in turn for those who were farther outside the orthodox fold than themselves. "Did they demand it equally for Baptists, Familists, Quakers, Antinomians, Fifth Monarchy Men, and all the 'fanatics' who were filling England with 'heresies,' many of them 'blasphemous' and some even 'immoral'? Where was the line to be drawn?" To the controversy concerning the various forms of church government and of worship was added in the years of the Civil War a controversy on Toleration. The number of pamphlets on the subject is legion. The controversy was not then and has never since been settled by reason. The knot was cut with the sword. After the King had been defeated at Marston Moor in the summer of 1644, the quarrel grew to a height between Manchester and Cromwell, the leaders respectively of the "orthodox" and the "sectarian" parts of the army. It was fought out in Parliament and ended in the triumph of Cromwell and the formation of the "New Model," an army formed on Cromwell's ideas, an army which by June, 1645 ended the "First Civil War" on the field of Naseby.

Presbyterian v. Congregational. The story of the next eight years is far too complex to follow even in outline; we can but mention the parties striving for political power. The King, a prisoner first to the Scots army, then to the English Parliament, and afterwards to the English army, always believed that he was more necessary to every party than they were to him, and died under the sentence of a High Court of Justice erected by a Parliament which had been purged under orders from the army. His justification came eleven years after, when his son returned to the throne. The English Parliament was Presbyterian for the most part except when overawed or purged by the army. Its ideal was an Established Presbyterian Church of England with-

The Political Period 1637—1677.

out toleration for any who differed therefrom. It remained in power until Ireland and Scotland had been conquered by the English Republic, and was then forcibly ejected by Cromwell because it wished to perpetuate itself. The Lowland Scots were Presbyterian and intolerant. They made a fatal blunder when they renewed the Civil War in 1648 on behalf of the King, a renewal which led directly to the King's death and to the conquest of their own country in 1650-1. Finally, the "New Model" army overawed the Parliament, and then in succession defeated the Scots and their English allies in 1648, brought about the trial and execution of "Charles Stuart" in 1649, conquered Ireland and Scotland (1649-51), and finally ejected the "Long Parliament" in 1653, leaving Cromwell, who had meanwhile become their General-in-Chief, in practical control of the State. The men who were neither Episcopalian nor Presbyterian had triumphed. They had appealed to the "Lord of Hosts" and He had answered them. They sang praises in the spirit of the Hebrew Psalmist to Him.

> *"Who remembered us at Dunbar: for His mercy endureth for ever;*
> *"Who remembered us at Worcester: for His mercy endureth for ever."*

Had He not, at Dunbar, arisen and the enemies been scattered? Was not Worcester a "crowning mercy"?

Oliver Cromwell. Dr. Gardiner has shewn that Cromwell's successful work was mainly negative. Episcopacy by Divine Right was struck down at Naseby, 1645, Presbyterianism by Divine Right with the ejection of the Long Parliament, 1653, Irish control over England was rendered impossible by the campaign of 1649, Scottish control by those of 1650-1. The field was now cleared for the advocates of Toleration in religious questions. What were they to do with their opportunity? Cromwell lived five and a half years after his accession to supreme

The Political Period 1637—1677.

political power, a period too short to establish anything on a firm basis, anything at least which was so revolutionary as that which he attempted in church matters. We have to consider therefore only proposals and tentative measures. But we see clearly that he was, in political ideas as well as those of religious doctrine, a thorough Calvinist. Men were by no means all equal. It was not fitting that the " ungodly " should have any share in the government of the reformed Church-State that was to be. He knew that Englishmen as a whole were not yet prepared to enter into the heritage which he and his army had gained for them. He therefore did not believe in the " people," nor would he trust the " fruits of " his army's " blood and travail " to the mercy of Parliaments, however carefully selected, who might " unlaw " one day what they had made law the previous. Such things as " liberty of conscience in religion " and " government by a Single Person and a Parlia-

A Primer of Free Church History.

ment" were to be "fundamental" laws, never to be changed.

The Nominated Parliament.
Cromwell believed, quite as much as Wentworth or Laud, in government by "men of light and leading"; but his ideas as to the necessary qualifications of such men differed from theirs. Accordingly a month after the Long Parliament had been ejected, Cromwell sent to the Congregational churches throughout the country asking them to supply nominations for a body which was to frame a constitution or form of government for the Church-State. The list thus furnished was revised by Cromwell and his officers, and those who were finally selected met in July, 1653. Among other changes, they proposed to abolish lay patronage and the payment of tithes, while they proposed the adoption of civil marriages and a State registration of births, marriages and deaths. These and other proposals of the "Barebones" or "Little Parliament," as this assembly came afterwards to be called,

The Political Period 1637—1677.

have either been since adopted, or are now regarded by many if not most as desirable. But in their own day, they were regarded as wildly revolutionary; they created such a storm among the clergy and the lawyers that the Parliament, in December, surrendered their power to Cromwell, and were dismissed to their homes.

The Church of England was therefore to be neither disestablished nor disendowed; the ideas of Roger Williams and the Baptists were not yet to prevail. But there were to be further changes made in the methods of its government and worship. As the Long Parliament of Henry VIII.'s reign had put an end to the authority of the Pope in England, as the Long Parliament of Charles I.'s reign had abolished the bishoprics, so now in 1653 the National Church was to receive the impress of the new rulers in the Commonwealth. In the "Instrument of Government," the document which Cromwell and his

Cromwell's State Church: (a) Creeds.

officers framed for the conduct of the Church-State, "the Christian religion as contained in the Scriptures" is the significantly short creed of the Established Church. "None were to be compelled to the public (i.e., established) profession by penalties or otherwise, but endeavours were to be used to win them by sound doctrine (teaching) and the example of a good conversation (behaviour)." Toleration was allowed to all who "profess faith in Jesus Christ" except "Papists, Episcopalians," those who "disturb the public peace" and "such as under the profession of Christ hold forth and practice licentiousness." In 1657 the form of government was further changed. In the new document, called the "Humble Petition and Advice," the creed is longer. "The true Protestant Christian religion, as contained in the Scriptures" is hereafter to be defined in a "Confession of Faith" to be drawn up by Protector and Parliament, which confession may not be

The Political Period 1637—1677.

"reviled or reproached maliciously or contemptuously, by opprobrious words or writing," and toleration is confined to those who believe in the Trinity and who "acknowledge the Holy Scriptures of the Old and New Testament to be the revealed Will and Word of God," exceptions also being made, as before, of Papists, Episcopalians, and "those who publish horrible blasphemies, or practise or hold forth licentiousness or profaneness under the profession of Christ." The "Confession of Faith" contemplated in this document took shape as "A Declaration of the Faith and Order owned and practised in the Congregational churches in England, Agreed upon and consented unto by their Elders and Messengers in their meeting at the Savoy, October 12th, 1658," during the brief rule of Richard Cromwell. It is a long document, elaborating in detail the system of Calvinistic theology, then almost universally held by English Puritans.

A Primer of Free Church History.

So far, therefore, as State documents go, we perceive a tendency to lengthen the creed and narrow the scope of the Established Church under Congregational rule. But the principle of toleration was never quite lost sight of, even by the clergy, and Oliver Cromwell was more tolerant than the system. The lay mind is generally more tolerant than the clerical, and he was bound, as ruler of the State, to look wider afield than the leaders of what were but a part of the community. The private use of the Episcopalian Prayer-Book was connived at, Quakers were, as far as possible, protected from prosecution, and Jews were allowed to settle in England after an absence of 350 years.

Cromwell's State Church: (b) Appointments.

What was the practical working of the scheme thus outlined? Ever since the outbreak of the Civil War, there had been maintained by the various governments of the country a Committee for the Ejectment of Scandalous Ministers. Many rectors and vicars had been by

The Political Period 1637—1677.

this committee and its agents ejected from their livings, some for immoralities of various kinds or neglect of duties, others for active opposition to the government of the day. Their places had been filled somewhat irregularly, and accordingly in March, 1654, Cromwell issued an Ordinance: "Whereas for some time there has been no certain course established for supplying vacant places, whereby the rights and titles of patrons have been prejudiced, it is hereby ordained that whoever shall be presented, nominated, chosen, or appointed to any benefice or lectureship shall be approved" by certain appointed "Triers" (i.e., examiners) "for the grace of God in him, his holy and unblameable conversation, as also for his knowledge and utterance." As there were several sub-commissions, there were different Triers for each county, and naturally they varied in the strictness and direction of their examinations, some being more narrow theologically than others.

A Primer of Free Church History.

Cromwell's State Church: (c) Illustrations.

How the system worked in detail may be best illustrated by two stories. In 1650, John Gifford formed a Congregational church in Bedford. In 1653 he was presented by the Mayor and Corporation to the rectory of St. John's in that town, and till 1660, the Congregational flock of which he was pastor worshipped in that parish church. In 1653, John Bunyan of Elstow joined the church. In 1655, John Gifford died, and the Congregational church appealed to Cromwell against the new presentation of the Mayor and Corporation. They gained their point for John Burton, their choice, was appointed by the Protector's authority. He died in 1660, and the church was then deprived of their "meeting house."

In 1643, Dr. Stamp, the Episcopalian vicar of Stepney, near London, was ejected "for being a proved prelatical innovator of Romish ceremonies, and a desperate malignant," and Dr. Hoyle, a Presbyterian, was appointed in his

The Political Period 1637—1677.

place. In 1644, Henry Burton, the rector of St. Matthew's, Friday Street, London, who had been in succession Episcopalian, Presbyterian and Congregationalist, founded a Congregational church in Stepney, of which William Greenhill, the Lecturer in the Parish church, became pastor. In 1653, Dr. Hoyle died and Greenhill became vicar of Stepney, his people using the parish church as their "meeting house" till 1660, when Greenhill was ejected, and was succeeded by Dr. Utye, an Episcopalian. These cases are typical of many others. Episcopalian incumbents were ejected, Presbyterians or Congregationalists took their places, received the tithes, conducted services in the parish churches, and ruled the parishes on Presbyterian or Congregational principles. The Court chaplains were Congregationalists. The Universities of Cambridge and Oxford were cleared of their "malignant" masters and fellows, college caps, gowns, and surplices went entirely out of fashion, but "sound learning and religious education" were never more zealously encouraged.

Baptists. In this State-Churchism of Oliver Cromwell, two classes of Englishmen refused to take part. We have already seen that Baptists were the first to advocate disestablishment as a principle and we find that now, when they could have taken advantage of the breadth of the National Church and could have had the advantages, social and pecuniary, of rectories and vicarages without changing their theology, forms of worship or church government, they still remained true to their first principles as to the relations of Church and State, and refused to take office in a church which was State established and endowed.

Quakers. But even the Baptists were outdone in "unorthodoxy" by a movement which arose in the years of the Commonwealth. In 1648 George Fox had come to the end of his internal conflicts and

The Political Period 1637—1677.

had started on the missionary journeys which lasted till the end of his life. Basing themselves on the "Light Within" which God gives to everyone who will receive it, he and his followers, the Society of Friends, were independent of all other means of grace. Bible, ministry, elders, all the "orderly" organisation which was regarded as of Divine Sanction by the other churches, became nothingness before the "enthusiasms" of the "Quakers." Defying thus not merely the State but the Church too as then all but universally conceived, the Quakers were the outcast of all men. And it must be confessed that the extravagances in which some of the early "Friends" indulged were enough to try the patience of most sober-minded Englishmen. Their refusal to take "lawful oaths," their denunciation of war, their refusal to remove their hats in any presence, their "prophesyings" against "steeple houses," not to speak of their deliberate neglect on some occasions of what are commonly regarded as the decencies of society caused them to be regarded as "lunatics" or "wilful disturbers of the peace," and they were "prosecuted" accordingly.

If therefore the Baptists refused to join with Cromwell's State Church, much more did "Quakers" refuse to touch the unclean thing.

Stuart Restoration. But the possibility of Baptists and Quakers even having anything to refuse rested on the power of the army and the ability of its great general to keep the discordant elements thereof in check. With Cromwell's death in September, 1658, anarchy came on the land, and within twenty months, England, to escape from anarchy, threw herself into the arms of the Stuart and Charles II. returned to the throne of his fathers. His first minister was Edward Hyde, Earl of Clarendon, a man of conservative views, who governed for seven years. England was for him still a theocracy, one State which was also to be

The Political Period 1637—1677.

one Church, in which therefore uniformity was as necessary in religious matters as in civil. In this view the Presbyterians and Congregationalists, though not, of course, the Baptists or Quakers, agreed with the minister. The difference betwen Clarendon and his Episcopalian friends on the one hand, and the more liberal of the Congregationalists on the other consisted in this, that the latter believed in "the Bible only" as the terms of the national creed and allowed a certain limited toleration to those who could not agree with them; while Clarendon and his friends believed that the creed should be longer and that to allow men to believe and act as they pleased in religious matters was quite as wrong as to allow endless diversity in matters of common civil concern.

Now it is quite evident that offices in the State, at least the more important, should be given only to those who approve of the principles on which the government is conducted. No one com- *The "System of Spoils," and the "Clarendon Code."*

plains that the leaders of the Opposition in Parliament are not in the Cabinet. In some countries, even to-day, the principle is extended to the holders of less important posts, and it was quite in the nature of things in the seventeenth century that the offices of Church and State, the livings in the Church, the fellowships at the Universities, the mayoralties and aldermanries of the chartered burghs should be held exclusively by Episcopalians when the King and Parliament had decided that Episcopacy and the Prayer-Book should be restored. We should therefore not let our quite modern ideas on religious liberty lead us rashly into surprise and indignation at the passing of the Corporation Act and the Act of Uniformity in 1661-2. As we saw earlier that Elizabeth and her ministers pursued what was then the "common-sense" method of governing so as to content the average population, so we must not blame the men of the Restoration for establish-

The Political Period 1637—1677.

ing their "narrow" principles of church government, just as the men of the Commonwealth had, by means of their triumphant army, established their "broad" church with its semi-tolerance. Congregationalists and Presbyterians were treated in 1660-7 much as they had treated Episcopalians in 1653--8. Each party in turn was the 'enemy' of the established government, believed to be dangerous, excluded from office and even from toleration on the same grounds as Roman Catholics are still debarred from certain privileges allowed to their Protestant, and even Jewish, fellow countrymen. If this thought is followed out, it will be seen that even the Conventicle Act of 1664, making all public worship unlawful except what was in accordance with the re-established Prayer-Book, is quite justifiable from the standpoint of contemporaries.

But, as we have said before, so much the more do we admire the courage, the devotion to truth, the martyr spirit of those who, because they could not in conscience submit to the new system, surrendered all, went out into the wilderness with the "Church of Christ," and even suffered imprisonment and exile for the sake of the Truth which was dearer to them than life itself. We do well to build Memorial Halls on the site of Fleet prisons, we do better to learn the story which these buildings commemorate, we do best when, besides "building the sepulchres of the prophets" we do what they did in their time, "go forward" towards the highest truths, truths higher than even they had grasped.

New England till 1783. Some of those who had returned from America now again crossed the Atlantic, and there were a few others who followed them. With the three thousand miles of salt water to protect them, the New England colonies were comparatively safe from those who with various motives attempted to con-

The Political Period 1637—1677.

trol them from England. Their paths were not entirely peaceful, and it is interesting to notice that in all schemes for the more effectual control of the colonies by the mother country in the seventeenth and eighteenth centuries, church questions are constantly mingled with matters of lay concern. Several attempts were made to introduce bishops into America, but they were resisted even by the Episcopalians of Virginia, and the colonies never had an episcopate of their own until they were certain, by British acknowledgment of their independence in 1783, that it was not part of a plan for the destruction of their other "liberties." When France was considering whether to help them in their revolt, part of the evidence studied for the purpose consisted of sermons by New England Congregationalists.

For seven years (1660-67), the Nonconformist churches in England and Scotland felt the full force of the storm

Pilgrim's Progress and Paradise Lost.

A Primer of Free Church History.

of persecution. We need not dwell on the sufferings of both clergy and laity. We note only two remarkable results. It is only through suffering that God evolves the best there is in man. It was not till Puritanism had gone through the trial of prosperity and then that of adversity that it produced the literary works that are to live for ever. When, owing to causes which we shall presently mention, the churches had a breathing space, there were written by Puritans of the Puritans two books that all Englishmen place to-day next to the Bible. John Bunyan, "brazier" and gospel preacher of Elstow, near Bedford, beguiled the weary months of his second imprisonment with writing "Pilgrim's Progress." John Milton, gentleman and scholar, Latin Secretary to the Commonwealth and Protectorate, pamphleteer, and advocate of the fullest liberty, "long choosing and beginning late," satisfied at length his longing "to write something which the

The Political Period 1637—1677.

world would not willingly let die," and dictated "Paradise Lost." When all that England has lost and gained by Puritanism comes in the future to be calmly weighed and measured one against the other, these additions to the soul-life of our nation will not be forgotten.

Chapter VI.

THE SUB-POLITICAL PERIOD 1667-1720.

The "Presbyterian or Independent Denomination."

When Clarendon fell in 1667, we enter on a period of 50 years which we may call the "sub-political" period of our history. The Nonconformist Churches of England are now fixed in their organisation. In their distress they have assimilated, for Presbyterians have of course lost the possibility of maintaining their interconnexion, while Congregational Churches, being less complex in their organisation, have suffered less in this way; the only difference between them is one of internal form. Congregationalists still hold by something of the original "Brownism" or democratic ideal, wherein the "Church meeting" has much power. Presbyterians give all the powers to the ministers and elders, who

The Sub-Political Period 1667—1720.

are therefore less controlled by the opinion of their flocks. So slight is this difference at first sight that the outside world confuses them together, and they are considered as one denomination, called indifferently "Presbyterian" or "Independent." Further, there are proposals for union, which are for a time carried into practice, but are later shipwrecked on theological differences.

But the "dissenting" or "nonconformist" churches still play a part in politics. Though their members are excluded from office, and tolerated only by connivance, they influence the action of the ecclesiastico-political parties of the day. These are three in number. The Roman Catholic, led by the Kings, Charles II. (1660-85) and James II. (1685-8), work surely, though at first carefully, through attempts at universal toleration towards the supremacy of their own church. The "High Church" party among the Episcopalians maintain the penal laws against

The Struggle between Catholic and Protestant.

A Primer of Free Church History.

Protestant dissenters, and acquiesce unwillingly in the dynastic changes that were made to secure the "Protestant Succession." The Low Church party in the Establishment regard the Protestant dissenters as their natural allies, are always promising to favour their interests and perform as much in that direction as is possible with a due regard to their own political objects. Thus, two of the three parties court the "Independents." The Roman Catholics, for their own ulterior ends are willing to grant them toleration as a temporary means to ultimate success; the Low Church party promise them due consideration if they will, as assuredly they must, support the "Protestant interest."

Declarations of Indulgence and the Toleration Act. In 1672, Charles II. issued a Declaration of Indulgence, under the terms of which persons and places were licensed for the public worship of Dissenters. Though the Parliament in the next year passed the Test Act and thus for-

The Sub-Political Period 1667—1720.

tified the Statutes which maintained the Episcopalian Church, that measure was directed more against Catholic than Protestant Dissenters. In 1687-8, James II. issued declarations similar to those of his brother, and so remodelled the corporations of the burghs which then elected the majority of the House of Commons, that they would in the coming General Election support the King in his attack on the "Clarendon Code." But that election was destined never to take place, for the Low Churchmen, joined on this occasion even by members of the High Church party, invited William of Orange, the husband of the heiress-presumptive to the throne, to come over and help them, and that Revolution was effected in England (1688-9) which has been called "glorious" and "Protestant." For their share in this policy the Protestant Dissenters were rewarded with the passing (1689) of a Toleration Act. The Test and Corporation Acts were not repealed, much less the Act of Uniformity, but the Conventicle Act was allowed to drop, and Protestant Dissenters might henceforth apply for licenses for public worship in certain houses on conditions prescribed.

Tory and Whig. In the reign of Anne (1702-14) the High Church party rose to power. Their period of influence is marked by the passing of the Occasional Conformity Act (1710) and the Schism Act (1713). The first of these was intended to prevent evasions of the Corporation Act by Dissenters who were in the habit of "conforming on occasion," i.e., of taking the Sacrament once according to the rites of the Established Church in order to qualify for municipal office. The Schism Act was intended to destroy the Academies which the Dissenters had founded to supply the want of a University education for their ministers. But when in 1714, by the death of Anne, the Low Church party came into power, both these Acts were soon repealed.

Chapter VII.

Religious Decadence.

By 1720, it was quite evident that England had passed away from the theocratic stage of her development. Religious questions were no longer the motives for political action. Protestant Episcopalians had secured their position in the Established Church as against their Protestant opponents in 1660-7, and against the Pope and his allies in 1688-9. The "Dissenters" had also secured legal toleration for themselves in 1689, and though the balance had slightly trembled in 1714, the accession of the Protestant Hanoverians had finally secured their peaceable enjoyment of rights to public worship. Protestant Episcopalians and Protestant Dissenters were both sheltered from their Roman Catholic opponents by their

"Hermit Crabs."

political friends the Whigs. For this protection they had to pay the price. The Convocations of the Established Church were practically suppressed for over a century, the patronage which was in the hands of government was used exclusively for party purposes and High Church principles were represented only among some of the "inferior clergy" or by the non-jurors, those who had refused to submit to the Protestant Revolution of 1688-9.

Indifference. Theologies and theocracies had passed from the arena of politics, and the average Englishman of the eighteenth century troubled himself no more about them. Hallam, writing his Constitutional History in 1827, is a good example of this attitude of mind with reference to the controversies of the seventeenth century. He is "the judicious Hallam," quite impartial, at least in intention, and without the least insight into the motives of his heroes. Lawyer-like, he regards the whole ques-

Religious Decadence.

tion as one of constitutional struggle; he thinks, if moderation had been used, no disturbance need have arisen, and, speaking of the suppression of the Convocation, the Parliament of the Anglican Church, says mockingly, "In the ferment of that age, it was expedient for the State to scatter a little dust over the angry insects: the Convocation was accordingly prorogued in 1717, and has never again sat for any business." How differently all earnest-minded people now think and speak of such things need not be said.

Nonconformists, too, were, so far .as politics were concerned, the humble hangers-on of the Whig party. Under the rule of Walpole (1720-42) it became an annual custom for Parliament to pass an Indemnity Act, forgiving Protestant Dissenters in municipal offices for the "crimes" they had committed against the Test and Corporation Acts during the previous twelve months, and their fate was sealed when Sir Robert

A Primer of Free Church History.

Walpole, in reply to their question when he would be able to grant them the privileges he professed himself willing yet so far unable to obtain for them, answered with the word "Never!"

Arianism and Deism. During the reigns of the first two Georges (1714-60) there was undoubtedly a real decadence in all religious life, and in this decline, so far as it is possible to know, Nonconformists had their share. Christianity was regarded as "reasonable"; all "enthusiasm" was sedulously avoided, and theological controversy was concerned mainly with two questions, closely connected. At first there was a growth of what was called "Arianism," "Socinianism," or "Unitarianism," which consisted mainly in a denial of the divinity of Jesus Christ. Its advocates were found both among Dissenters and in the Established Church. In the Dissenting churches we note a remarkable divergence. Unitarians, whether educated at Congregational or Presbyterian

Religious Decadence.

"academies," tended to seek office in Presbyterian churches rather than Congregational or Baptist. They were more independent of the opinion of their people in the former than in the latter, and being more generally endowed, they were enabled to preach on to pews more and more empty till the congregations had in many instances all but vanished. The more "popular" government of Congregationalist churches prevented this change of opinion on the part of their pastors. In the theological developments of the eighteenth century, we thus find the reason for the fact that Congregational churches are mainly Trinitarian in doctrine, while many Unitarian churches can historically describe themselves as Presbyterian.

The other theological discussion of those times arose out of an attack on all Divine Revelation. Deists or Theists, as they were called, denied the possibility of miracles and the truth of Chris-

A Primer of Free Church History.

tianity in general; it was against thinkers of this kind, such as David Hume, that Butler wrote his "Analogy of Religion, Natural and Revealed, to the Constitution and the Course of Nature" (1736), and Paley, his "Evidences of the Christian Religion" (1794).

Decay of Discipline. The battle was nobly fought, and the victory remained with "those who believed," but the endeavour to be "reasonable" seemed to have cost the churches all their vitality. Theology was saved, but all religion except a respectable morality seems to have been lost; the idea of the Christian Church as a State or government of men died away. Between the established and the tolerated claimants on the allegiance of the population, many refused obedience to all ecclesiastical rule, and the consequence has been the total absence from modern minds even of the conception of church discipline. The various Churches now attempt only to persuade; the times

Religious Decadence.

when an Established Church could enforce attendance by the infliction of fines or imprisonment, and Nonconformist Churches by threats of excommunication for " disorderly walking " seem now to have passed away for ever. They are regarded as belonging to the " dark ages " of " superstition."

Chapter VIII.

THE EVANGELICAL REVIVAL.

Wesley, and the Effects of his Teaching.

The story of the revival of religion in England begins in 1739, with the itinerant preaching of the brothers John and Charles Wesley and of George Whitfield, all of Oxford University, whose manifold activity had several consequences. Owing to the inelasticity at that time of the parochial system of the Established Church and to the working of the Toleration Act, what was intended to be a society subsidiary to the parish churches was forced into becoming a great accession to Dissent. Owing to differences between the Wesleys and Whitfield, theological controversy was revived between Arminians and Calvinists; and "Methodism," as the new movement was nicknamed, divided into three or

The Evangelical Revival.

four bodies which exist to our own day. But with all these regrettable divisions, Wesleyanism has had a lasting effect on the whole of Christian England; an Evangelical party arose in the Established Church and the older Dissenting churches were quickened into life. One of the signs of the revival was the outbreak of the militant churches into song. To eighteenth century congregations, used to unpoetical paraphrases of the psalms, such hymns as Wesley's "Jesu, lover of my soul," "Hark, the herald angels sing," and Watts' "When I survey the wondrous Cross," "Come let us join our cheerful songs," came as a welcome relief. Even the keen partisan, Toplady, could express his Calvinism in the ever-popular "Rock of ages cleft for me."

The ideal of the Evangelicals was to further individual piety by the salvation of souls and thus to Christianise the State. They were comparatively indifferent to church organisation in it-

Evangelicalism.

self, and both Episcopalians and Dissenters united in the foundation of the London Missionary Society in 1795, and of the British and Foreign School Society in 1807.

The Evangelical Revival had, however, political effects before long. Not to dwell on minor changes of the law the details of which are tedious, the most important events of this kind were the repeal of the Test and Corporation Acts in 1828, and the Act for the Relief of Roman Catholics from Political Disabilities forced on the government of Wellington and Peel in 1829 by the Irish agitation.

The Modern State: National, not Theocratic. The advance towards religious liberty and equality was due not only to the revival of religious affairs; we must attribute it partly to the spirit of the age. The reforming monarchs of the latter half of the eighteenth century, Frederick the Great of Prussia, Joseph II. of Austria, and others, pushed forward the idea of the State as the uniting motive

The Evangelical Revival.

of countries in contradistinction to the Church; the thorough-going advocates of the Romish theocracy, the Jesuits, were suppressed even by the Roman Catholic monarchs of the Bourbon family, and the French Revolution changed ideas throughout all Europe, as well as the institutions of France. The Whigs in England of the years 1815-32 had, as we have seen in the example of Hallam, no respect for the Church, in comparison with the State. It is out of such ideas as these that the belief in the possibility of religious liberty and equality without danger and even with profit to the State came to be a maxim of practical politics.

When, by the example of the United States of America, and by the growth of the idea of nationality, it began to be seen that religious unity and uniformity were not necessary to maintain the unity and safety of the State, it was possible for the idea of "disestablishment" to take root in the minds of statesmen.

A Primer of Free Church History.

The Church was spoken of as a department of the civil service, the clergy, both Established and Dissenting, were regarded only as a superior kind of police, helping the State to discharge what were then regarded as its only legitimate functions, those of protection from force and fraud. The churches were of the same way of thinking as most people of their time, in regarding individual enterprise as the best method of attaining results.

"Religious Liberty and Equality" defined.
"Religious liberty" may be defined as absolute freedom for each individual to unite, if he pleases, with any others, like-minded with himself, in any church or religious organisation. Thus described, religious liberty is compatible with an Established Church; but if the definition be enlarged, as it would be by many, so as to include on the one hand freedom from compulsion to contribute towards the expenses of churches or religious organisations with which the individual does not agree, or on the other,

The Evangelical Revival.

the freedom of all churches or religious organisations from outside control, then "religious liberty" would be incompatible with the existence of Established Churches. It is in these latter senses that the phrase is generally used to-day, and that it is connected so closely with the word "equality." "Religious equality" does not of course mean, as some have somewhat perversely supposed, the equality of all religions, but the equality of all persons before the law with respect to their religious beliefs.

"Religious liberty and equality," according to the larger definition, have never existed in any European country; it is doubtful if before this century they have been the program of any religious body; certainly, of no political party. We have noticed earlier instances of their advocacy, and even of their adoption in the New World, but the Liberals of 1820-1832, owing partly to the increased religious zeal which was the consequence of the Evangelical re-

A Primer of Free Church History.

vival, partly to the views as to relationships between Church and State which we have just briefly indicated, began to speak of disestablishing the English National Church.

Chapter IX.

THE CATHOLIC REVIVAL.

Tractarianism.

The proposals for disestablishment which were made about 1830, forced a party to assert themselves, who had already been feeling their way to other ideas. They had founded for instance the "National Society for the Education of the Poor in the Principles of the Church of England" (1811), and were reviving in the nineteenth century the conceptions of the Christian Church as an institution different from and possibly antagonistic to the State, at least such a State as was developing tendencies towards disestablishment and disendowment under Liberal auspices.

The bishops had been told "to put their house in order." It was time to seek some other basis for the Church than the good-humoured patronage

A Primer of Free Church History.

given to the Episcopalians or the still more contemptuous toleration accorded to the Dissenters. When the Test and Corporation Acts had been repealed (1828), not from a high sense of duty or justice, but because they had become scandalous relics of a " barbarous " age, it was necessary to realise once again the claims of a Divine institution that was greater far than the mere expediencies of governments and cabinets. The movement began among some Oxford clergymen whose ideal was a church founded on the Apostles and maintaining its continuity through the ages by means of the threefold ministry of bishops, priests and deacons. In the Tractarian movement, as it was called because it began with a series of ninety "Tracts for the Times," much came to be heard, as in Laud's generation, of priests, altars, and sacrifices, and of " apostolic succession." Some of the leaders and many of their followers, failing to find in an Established Church

The Catholic Revival.

the ideal of their dreams, naturally drifted to the great non-established episcopal church whose head was the bishop of Rome. Ritual was exalted, and, as the appeal was to antiquity, we heard much of going "behind the Reformation."

Now all this was extremely alarming to Evangelical Dissenters—"Shall we go back to Rome?" was the cry—and in the hatred of the sacerdotalism and clericalism that was associated with the movement, Nonconformists did not at first see the living force within: the conception of the Church of Christ which was being recalled to life out of the dormancy of a hundred years. But, after a time, the essential idea seized also on the more enlightened among ourselves, and whereas we were content to be called "chapel" people in contrast to "Church" folk, we are now beginning to realise that we too are churches, real members of Christ's Holy Catholic Church, having a real

Nonconformist Churches.

A Primer of Free Church History.

"apostolic succession" as distinct from the artificial, official, succession of our brethren. We too "have an altar," we also are a royal priesthood, being "kings and priests unto God." We too offer "sacrifices," and we are beginning to hark back to antiquity, first the antiquity of the seventeenth century, when we were large sharers in the national life and even for a time had the mastery in the Established Church. But more than that, we claim a share in the most ancient of Christian antiquity, the Apostolic age, and we claim that the records of the New Testament lend themselves as well to the Nonconformist theories as to the Episcopalian. Though we do not claim an exclusive Divine Sanction (as our forefathers did) for our own forms of polity, yet we refuse to be un-churched by those who insist on a rigid acceptance of their own procedure. We recognise the Christianity of all who love the Lord Jesus Christ in sincerity, leaving to all full liberty

The Catholic Revival.

to unite churches in Presbyterian or Episcopalian methods if so it like them. We, more than any others, are "Catholic"-minded, and would refuse to enter into the "communion of saints" with none who are willing to fraternise with us. We recognise unity in diversity, and see no need, in order to effect a real "union of Christendom," to acknowledge Episcopates, historic or other, as the only method of connection among fellow-Christians.

Chapter X.

THE PRESENT DAY.

British Industry and British Empire.
The last century and a half have seen two changes in the condition of our country, to which the word "great" seems scarely adequate. Since the middle of the last century, owing to the invention of machinery and the discovery of the uses of steam, the whole of our social fabric has been completely revolutionised. When George III. ascended the throne in 1760, Great Britain was an agricultural country, though possessing some towns of importance as centres of trade and industry. When his grand-daughter began to reign in 1837, it had become a manufacturing country, its population for the most part gathered together in factory towns of ever increasing size, and depending for their daily food on the regularity of supplies from abroad.

The Present Day.

When Victoria was crowned, she reigned over Australia and large tracts of country in America, besides scattered territories in Africa, the East and West Indies, but for the most part these were scarcely known, much less inhabited, by persons of European descent. Now that sixty years have passed, we in England are beginning to realise that we are but a part of a world-wide empire, each division of which has interests and claims.

The Churches in Arrear. This growth and shifting of the population began at the time when the churches were in their lowest and most torpid condition; it had progressed far before they had roused themselves sufficiently to cope with the problem thus presented. They were therefore heavily handicapped, if we may use the expression, and they have not even yet made up their "lee-way." Attempts made a few years ago at collecting statistics suddenly revealed to the Christian Churches that, whatever their respective figures might be, they were, all taken together, but a fraction of the community, both in actual numbers and in accommodation for public worship. The story of the 19th century, therefore, is not that of a population all at least nominally Christian though divided as to doctrines and forms of church government, but of a population indifferent to, largely ignorant of, Christian teaching, in the midst of which all the churches are striving, with a rivalry which is to a large extent friendly, to win those who have been lost through neglect.

Missionary Societies. The Societies for Promoting Christian Knowledge and for the Propagation of the Gospel in Foreign Parts were founded quite at the beginning of the 18th century by members of the Established Church Their spheres of work were mainly, if not entirely, confined to the British dominions.

A hundred years later, missionary societies began to be formed with a

The Present Day.

larger scope. The "Baptist" was founded in 1792, the "London" in 1795, the "Church" in 1799, and since then their number has grown, and their area of operations now embraces the world.

It is a platitude that a church which does not missionise is almost an anomaly, and can scarcely be regarded as a real church at all. And conversely, the foundation of missions tends at once to revive the energies of a church in all parts of its activity.

This century therefore has seen, with the growth of the population, continual efforts on the part of the Free Churches as well as those of the Established, to keep step with that growth, and to make up for arrears. One necessary result has been an increase in the number of denominations, though we are learning now, both in theory and practice, that they are but denominations in the literal sense of the word, mere names

A Primer of Free Church History.

denoting no serious difference in what we agree in regarding as the fundamentals of the Christian faith.

New Denominations. Of these names, the most important are the Calvinistic Methodists of Wales dating at least from 1743, the Methodist New Connexion founded in 1797, the United Methodist Free Churches who held their first assembly in 1857, the Primitive Methodists whose first conference was held in 1820, and the Bible Christians originating about the same time, strong, mainly in the south-western counties.

A word must also be given to Scottish ecclesiastical history since the Revolution of 1688 "established" in Scotland the ancient Presbyterian Kirk. We have no space to speak of the various secessions of the 18th century, but all the world knows of the great "Disruption" of 1843, which divided Presbyterian Scotland into the "Established" and the "Free" Church. These two and the "United Presbytery" are the larg-

The Present Day.

est bodies which represent modern Scottish Presbyterianism.

The influx of Scotsmen into England has given rise to another body, the "Presbyterian Church of England," consisting partly, specially in the north of England, of old Presbyterian churches dating from the 17th century, and partly of new churches formed mainly to meet the requirements of young Scotsmen migrating southwards. It is in communion with the Free Church of Scotland.

Federation and Expansion.

It will be noted that all these movements, Methodist of various kinds, and others, are Presbyterian in their form of church government. The tendency in this century is towards federation. We see it in politics and in business, and it is therefore not surprising to find it also in ecclesiastical life. Even the Congregationalists and Baptists have abandoned the "independency" of the 17th century, and are grouping themselves into Unions of various kinds, county and

A Primer of Free Church History.

national. The Baptist Union was formed in 1813, the Congregational in 1831. In 1892, a movement began to take shape, the effect of which it is too early to forecast with accuracy, but the possibilities of which are infinite. In that year the first conference was held under the auspices of the National Council of Free Churches.

All these movements in old England have their counterparts in the British Colonies, where the non-episcopal churches have taken their due share in the life of the community. In these parts of the British empire, we may not call them "Free Churches," for the words "nonconformist" and "dissenter" have no meaning in Greater Britain; there is no established church. Much more do these remarks apply to the United States of America where, by the first amendment to the Constitution, "Congress shall make no law respecting an establishment of religion, or prohibiting the free exercise thereof," and

The Present Day.

where none of the States' legislatures have established any form of religion.

Of the many voluntary activities for the social amelioration of the people of England in which members of the Free Churches have borne their share of their contribution towards State methods of accomplishing the same work, there is neither need nor space to speak. But on the particular question of Elementary School Education, we may say a few words.

The British and Foreign School Society was founded by Evangelicals of the Established and Nonconformist churches in 1807. The "National Society" was founded by Anglicans in 1811. Both societies were voluntary, working for the same aim in rival ways. In 1833, the State began to supplement their resources by grants from the Budget, and this was increased at different periods.

Elementary Education.

In 1870, the Elementary Education Act made arrangements for an entirely

State-established and State-endowed system of elementary education which was to supplement the work of the voluntary societies and other similar agencies.

Since that year, therefore, there has been a two-fold rivalry between the Evangelical and the "Catholic" educators; their "voluntary" schools have earned more and more of "government grants," and there has arisen an ecclesiastico-political contest at the election of the various "School Boards," somewhat similar to the conflicts of the 17th century. But into all the ramifications of this contest, including the question of training colleges and village education, we must not enter.

Removal of Disabilities. During this century, many grievances from which our forefathers suffered have been redressed. The protection afforded by the Toleration Act was extended in 1779 and 1813. The Test and Corporation Acts were re-

The Present Day.

pealed in 1828 and 1866. Roman Catholics obtained relief in 1829. Compulsory Church Rates were abolished in 1868. The Universities and their privileges were opened to us by Acts of 1854, 1856, 1871, and 1882, and much has been gained towards an equal treatment in the matter of marriages and burials. The "Irish Church" was disestablished and disendowed in 1869, but this was done because the case of that church was exceptional. It was and always had been the church of a small minority. The "Church of Scotland," and of "England and Wales," are still established, because British politicians shape their conduct, not by the logic of theories, but by the play of political forces. They are all, in a very real sense of the word, opportunists.

What, then, is the present ecclesiastical condition in England? After fifty years of the "Oxford Movement," we see two forces arrayed, one against the other, in the Established Church. One *[High Church v. Low Church.]*

A Primer of Free Church History.

proclaims that church to be a branch of the Catholic Church, not Protestant, and differing from the "Catholic" churches of the Continent only in refusing obedience to the Pope, and in a number of beliefs and practices varying according to the belief and practice of the theorist. Many of this party apparently wish to minimise these differences.

The other party proclaims as loudly that the "National Church" is "Protestant," that the changes made at the "Reformation" were large and valuable, and that their opponents are "Romish" in tendency if not in fact.

Even if the Church in which these disputes have arisen were a "free" church like ourselves, we should be interested in the controversy, and, whether we agreed with the "history" set forth by one side or the other, our sympathies would of course be for those who are battling for the Protestantism

The Present Day.

for which we ourselves have long suffered a kind of semi-martyrdom.

But the Church which doubts whether it is "Catholic" or "Protestant" is an established church, its endowments are, as we believe, derived directly or indirectly from State authority, and we are, by law, members thereof. Therefore we all have a still more immediate interest in its differences. We claim the right to speak and act in the matter, just as the Separatists in the 17th century took part in the ecclesiastico-political conflicts of their day.

Indeed, the present situation resembles, in a very remarkable degree, the position of affairs in 1640. Then, as now, there were two parties in the Established Church to which we may apply the term "High Church" and "Low Church." Then, as now, there were Englishmen, outside the established church, yet intensely interested in its welfare. The ecclesiastical conditions are startlingly alike.

A Primer of Free Church History.

The political conditions are different; the relations of King and Parliament are quite otherwise than those of the 17th century; we possess institutions, such as the Cabinet, and the broad suffrage, which did not exist two hundred and fifty years ago. But it ought not to be difficult to forecast the course of the story, sufficiently at least to give us wisdom for the struggle.

Disestablishment. One only of the thoughts that naturally arise can be touched here. The High Church party have more or less openly rebelled against the control of the State. Though they shrink from using the word, they are in favour of disestablishment. The Low Church party are beginning to say that if their opponents win in the political conflict, disestablishment will be the only way out of the difficulty.

Thus, the stress of theological strife is tending to bring about what we, as free churches, have advocated, quite practically, and, to a large extent, theo-

The Present Day.

retically, for a long time. Our sympathies in this matter are entirely with those who are ecclesiastically at the opposite pole from ourselves.

On this matter, all members of our free churches should, in proportion to their capacity, see clearly and act firmly. Our national history has taught us, with superabundance of proof, what an influence for evil, all the greater because so subtle, the possession of political power has on any branch of the Christian Church. We believe thoroughly in disestablishment as its inherent right.

But this ecclesiastico-political belief is, with us, a secondary matter compared with the root principle of our Evangelical faith. This foundation, next to belief in Jesus Christ, is that every human soul should come into immediate contact with God, that even for the weakest and most ignorant, it is necessary to avoid all human mediation save by way of instruction and guidance. This is the keynote to the history of the Free

Sacerdotalism

A Primer of Free Church History.

Churches of England; this is the principle which inspired them to do and dare all they did and suffered for the sake of the truth.

The eternal struggle between sacerdotal views of religion and its opposite is still with us. It was in the Jewish Church, it has been in the Christian Church from its very beginning. There is no greater problem, none more difficult for the human mind to solve, than the reasons for this continual conflict. We cannot even touch its fringe in these pages; it should form the subject of our earnest prayer and thought in later years.

Summary We have thus traced, in briefest outline, the story of Protestant Free Churches in England from the 16th century till the present day. But we must not forget that there has been during all this period a free church in England which is not Protestant in any sense. When Elizabeth decided to reject the Papal Supremacy, the Roman Catho-

The Present Day.

lics became dissenters, and have continued so to exist till this day. They, too, have had their martyrs and their difficulties. For many years they were unable to maintain their system in any but the most maimed condition, and it was not till 1850 that English Roman Catholics were again governed by bishops taking their titles from English towns. Since that date, in spite of an Act of Parliament, passed in panic and ever since a dead letter, Roman Catholicism has been a fully organised church in England. With this omission thus briefly supplied, we can summarise the story of this primer.

In the reign of the Tudors, Christian England divided into a Papal and a National Church. The former was reformed, with the other Papal churches, by the Council of Trent, the latter by successive Acts of Parliament and of Convocation. Almost immediately, if not simultaneously, non-Papal Englishmen were divided into those who wished

A Primer of Free Church History.

to reform still further, and those who were content with the reform accomplished by Elizabeth. Of the ultra-reformers, some were content to remain within the Established Church and hope for better times; these were the Puritans of the 16th and 17th centuries. Others separated entirely from the Established Church, and erected free churches, which were, like the Roman Catholics, "persecuted" by the Anglican authorities. These were the Congregationalists and Baptists.

Early in the 17th century, many free churchmen fled from persecution to the Netherlands and America, though some of them stayed at home, specially Baptists. In the thirties of the century, theological and liturgical controversies rose to such a height within the Established Church, that many of the Puritans emigrated to America and founded there Congregational Established Churches. In the time of the Civil War and Commonwealth there

The Present Day.

were endless developments—theological, liturgical, and disciplinary; the multiplicity of sects in those years is more than can be dealt with in these pages. We have dealt briefly with the rise and fall of Presbyterianism and of Congregationalism in England. The result in 1660 was that Protestant Episcopacy was again established, Roman Catholics, Presbyterians, Congregationalists, Baptists and Quakers were "persecuted."

Then, partly owing to political developments, partly to weariness of strife, all English churches fell for a time into apathy, and the "philosophical" spirit of the 18th century led some of the older churches into Unitarianism. Against this apathy the Wesleys led a movement of revival, and thus not only have the older sects survived into the 19th century but they have been joined on the one hand by Unitarians, and on the other by the various branches of "Methodism" and its imitators.

A Primer of Free Church History.

Among the various movements of our own age, we have remarked the increase of religious life in all the churches, the "Catholic" revival in the Established Church, the ever-growing activity of the Evangelical churches, the interest taken in social questions and the endeavours to win the "lapsed millions" for the Christian Church. This energy has of course given rise to rivalry between the churches, much of which is friendly, but some of which is otherwise.

Conclusion. The author of the Epistle to the Hebrews, seeking for illustrations of the effects of faith, finds himself drawn into a sketch of the history of his nation. We English, too, if only our eyes were opened to see, could write a similar history of our own country. More perhaps even than the Hebrew, we can name heroes who "have endured seeing Him who is invisible." "The time would fail" us also "to tell of" those who, in our own country, as in Israel of old, "through faith subdued kingdoms,

The Present Day.

wrought righteousness, obtained promises, quenched the violence of fire, escaped the edge of the sword, out of weakness were made strong, waxed valiant in fight. . . . Others had trial of mockings and scourgings, yea, moreover, of bonds and imprisonment . . . being destitute, afflicted, tormented."

"Wherefore, seeing we also are encompassed about with so great a cloud of witnesses, let us lay aside every weight, and the sin that doth so easily beset us."

The earnest hope of the author, and the purpose with which this primer is written, is to stir young Free Churchmen, firstly, to read the history of their forefathers in the faith, then to soak themselves in the story till they are permeated with its spirit; finally, to go deeper and deeper in research and reflection till they learn the wisdom of the ages, and so become mental and spiritual heirs of those who have gone before us.

A Primer of Free Church History.

Let us beware of the temptations that surround us, even in our best of times. By all means add to worship all that will help us to approach the Father of our Spirits in spirit and in truth, but let us not be misled by outward beauty to miss the inward and spiritual graces of which these are but the outward and visible signs.

Let us not forget, in the attractions which are prepared for those who are outside the Kingdom, that these baits are not the proper food of the members of Christ's Church. Let us realise more and more what is meant when we say that the Christ is our King, and the Church His means of rule. In a word, let us leave the "beggarly elements," and go on, strengthened by discipline, individual and collective, to attain all the higher possibilities of Christian Church life.

Not till we realise that we are not only free, but churches, shall we be able to speak with our enemies in the gate.

The Present Day.

Not till we realise the full possibilities of an organised church-life, shall we derive the strength that should come from a sentiment of union with the past, of triumphant endeavour in the present, or of well-founded hope for the future.

A BRIEF BIBLIOGRAPHY.

The following books are mentioned, not because they are exhaustive of the subject, but because they have for the most part been read, and all of them been at least consulted by the author :—

DEXTER : "Congregationalism." 1865. A useful set of lectures on the subject, with an enormous Bibliography attached.

DRYSDALE : "History of Presbyterians in England." 1889. A well-written book, and useful.

EVANS : "The Early English Baptists." 2 vols. 1862. Old-fashioned and too wordy. A new history of the Baptists in a desideratum.

HANBURY : "Historical Memorials relating to the Independents or Congregationalists." 3 vols. 1839.
The work of a violent partisan, but useful because it consists mainly of long extracts from Congregationalist pamphlets, with occasional quotations from their opponents, which are useful when taken out of Hanbury's context.

MATHER : "Magnalia Christi Americana." The Ecclesiastical History of New England. 1702. Would that it could be reprinted !

MILTON : "Prose Works." 5 vols. (Bohn). Vol. II. is specially interesting.

Of modern books written from the purely historical standpoint, we may mention, among others, these :—

ARBER : "Story of the Pilgrim Fathers." 1897.

——— "Introductory Sketch to the Martin Marprelate Controversy." 1880.

BROWN: John Bunyan ; "His Life, Times, and Work." 1885.

——— "The Pilgrim Fathers of New England and their Puritan Successors." 1895.

GARDINER : "History of England." (1603-42). 10 vols. 1884.

——— "History of the Great Civil War." 3 vols. 1886-91.

——— "History of the Commonwealth and Protectorate." 1894-7.

——— "Student's English History." Vol. II. 1897.

HATCH : "The Organisation of the Early Christian Churches." 1882.

HODGKIN : "George Fox." 1896.

MACKENNAL : "Story of the English Separatists." 1893.

MASSON : "Life of Milton in connection with the History of his Time." 6 vols. 1880.

The following may also be mentioned, though many are out of print.

T. ARMITAGE: "History of the Baptists." 30/- 1887. U.S.A.

H. S. BURRAGE: "History of Anabaptists in Switzerland." 1882. U.S.A.

W. CATHCART: "Baptists and the American Revolution." 1876. U.S.A.

E. R. CONDER: "Why are we Dissenters?" 1/- 1881.

J. HUNT COOKE: "Manual of Baptism."

J. M. CRAMP: "Baptist History." 5/- 1871.

R. W. DALE: "Manual of Congregational Principles." 1/6. 1884.

J. J. GOABY: "Bye-paths of Baptist History." 4/- 1871.

D. C. HAYNES: "History of Baptist Denomination." 1875. U.S.A.

F. J. A. HORT's: "Christian Ecclesia." 1897.

J. B. JOHNSON: "Our Principles, &c." 9d. 1876.

G. T. LADD: "Princples of Church Polity" (Congregational). 1882. U.S.A.

J. M. PENDLETON: "Three Reasons Why I am a Baptist." 1884. U.S.A.

S. T. PORTER: "Independency." 6/- 1856.

GEO. PUNCHARD: "View of Congregationalism." 1865. U.S.A.

H. R. REYNOLDS : " Ecclesia." 1871.

A. H. ROSS : " The Church Kingdom." 12/6. 1888. U.S.A.

SKEAT's & MIALL's " History of the Free Churches of England " (1688-1891). 1892.

W. TALLACK : " Geo. Fox, the Friends and Early Baptists." 1868. U.S.A.

ROB. VAUGHAN : " English Nonconformity." 7/6. 1862.

H. C. VENNER : " Short History of the Baptists." 1898.

F. WAYLAND : " Principles and Practices of Baptist Churches." 1861. U.S.A.

W. R. WILLIAMS : " Lectures on History of the Baptists." 1877. U.S.A.

IT IS A SIGN OF THE TIMES THAT SO MUCH IS BEING DONE FOR THE CHILDREN.

Crown 8vo, cloth, 3s. 6d., with complete index.

Sermons to Boys and Girls

BY JOHN EAMES, B.A.

"These addresses display considerably more culture than the majority of sermons to young people. They have attractive titles, and the style is simple. They would, we imagine, be listened to with interest by intelligent children on a Sunday afternoon."—*S. S. Chron.*

"This collection of Sermons, all of them brief, pithy, and practical, appeals to many beside the young, though from their plainness and simplicity they are specially suited to those for whom they were intended."—*Family Churchman.*

"Beautifully printed and bound. Subjects aptly chosen, interestingly handled, and the addresses abound in happy illustration."—*Christian Commonwealth.*

"Preaching to children is now a common practice. Mr. Eames has given us a volume of 'sermonettes,' which are well worthy of publication, simple, pointed, and full of apt illustration. They would be pleasant to listen to and furnish good reading."—*Freeman.*

"Mr. Eames takes pains to be interesting, and uses sensible illustrations, keeping clear of questionable anecdotage."—*Christian World.*

"Many a preacher to children might well take a leaf out of Mr. Eames's book. The subjects are well chosen, and the style of treatment eminently appropriate."—*Christian Age.*

"Sermon literature for young people, whether to be read directly by them, or embodied in pulpit teaching for their benefit, is a useful and growing class. Many will welcome 'Sermons to Boys and Girls,' which contains fifteen discourses pointed and well constructed. The index gives a list of the many anecdotes and illustrations that brighten the pages."—*The Christian.*

"Mr. Eames's discourses are examples of what children's addresses ought to be—simple in language but pointed in teaching."—*Methodist Times.*

"May be read with interest."—*Literary World.*

"There is considerable freshness both in selection of texts and their treatment. The get-up is very tasteful."—*Primitive Methodist.*

"We heartily commend Mr. Eames's volume to all preachers to children, and should imagine it will be a welcome possession in many homes."—*Light and Leading.*

LONDON: H. R. ALLENSON, 30, PATERNOSTER ROW, E.C.

A CHOICE GIFT FOR A BUSY CHRISTIAN WORKER.

Neat Cloth, 394 *pages*. *Crown 8vo.*, 5s., *Post free.*

Seed Corn for . . The Sower

Or Thoughts, Themes and Illustrations . .

BY

Rev. C. PERREN, D.D.

The Methodist Times says :—"An admirable collection of thoughts and illustrations, compiled for the use of Christian workers. One of the charms of this book is the absence of the stock illustrations, common to works of this class. The value of the work is enhanced by the fact that the subjects are arranged in alphabetical order, and there are two exhaustive indexes, one of authors and the other of texts. Rightly used, the book will be a boon to preachers and teachers."

The Christian World says :—"The book is everywhere bright and readable, and hard-pressed speakers whose ideas need reinforcement will often find here what they are in search of."

The Christian says :—"'Seed Corn' answers well to its secondary title, as a volume of 'Thoughts, Themes and Illustrations for the Pulpit and Platform, and for Home Reading.' A good sower will know how to use this seed-corn."

The Literary World says :—"Some workers will find it serviceable. The Indexes of Authors, Texts, and Subjects will aid those who are in search of the kind of help which the book can give."

The Sunday School Chronicle says :—"Dr. Perren's 'Seed Corn' is a good and useful book. It contains many thoughts, themes, parables and similitudes. Gleanings from the vineyards and harvest fields of a ministry which has lasted for more than a quarter of a century, which God has acknowledged and blessed. The most original of us may learn from these pages."

SEED CORN FOR . . THE SOWER

Is arranged in alphabetical order throughout, and is equipped with the following three good indexes :

   Complete Index of Texts Illustrated.
   Complete Index of 250 Authors quoted.
   Complete Index of Subjects treated.

Thus making its contents easily available.

5/-

LONDON: H. R. ALLENSON, 30, PATERNOSTER ROW, E.C.

PHILLIPS BROOKS' NOTABLE BOOKS.

Lectures on Preaching. By the Right Rev. Phillips Brooks. Neat cloth, uniform with Phillips Brooks's Works, issued by Messrs. Macmillan. Crown 8vo, 5s.

"Mr. Allenson has done very well to let us have it in uniformity with the other books by Phillips Brooks which we possess. It is a book of permanent value."—*Expository Times.*

"These valuable lectures constitute a really great book."—*The Baptist.*

"Readers of these noble and impassioned pages will be at no loss to discover wherein lay Dr. Phillips Brooks' secret of power."—*The Speaker.*

"Well worth reading and re-reading by young clergy. They can hardly study the great preacher's methods without learning much, very much to help and strengthen them."—*Church Times.*

"We have more than once commended this delightful book. There is no preacher of the Gospel, there is hardly any public speaker on any subject, who can read any one of these lectures without learning something profitable. We only wish all our preachers could own, and make their own, the sterling truth of this delightful and valuable book."—*Methodist Times.*

"There is no book of Homiletics more worthy of earnest and prayerful study."—*Independent.*

The Influence of Jesus on the Moral, Social, Emotional, and Intellectual Life of Man. By the Right Rev. Phillips Brooks. Uniform with "Lectures on Preaching." Crown 8vo, 5s.

"The Influence of Jesus is theologically the most characteristic of all Bishop Brooks' works. If one would understand this man, one must read this book. Mr. Allenson has given us a new and attractive edition."—*Expository Times.*

"A book which might well become popular. Bishop Brooks' logic was always lighted up by imaginative power, and his strongest reasoning was tremulous with emotion. The purpose of the book is established with an irresistible force of logic and a wealth of choice illustration. The reissue of the book is altogether timely."—*Baptist Magazine.*

Essays and Addresses. By Right Rev. Phillips Brooks. Religious, Literary, and Social. Edited by the Rev. John Cotton Brooks. Crown 8vo, cloth, 2 vols. Sold separately. Vol. I., Religious Topics; Vol. II., Social and Literary. 5s. each.

These Essays have hitherto only been issued at 8s. 6d. net.

Letters of Travel (1865-1890). By Right Rev. Phillips Brooks. This book has been transferred to Mr. Allenson by Messrs. Macmillan, and from having hitherto been published at 8s. 6d. net is now re-issued at the more popular price of 5s., subject to usual discount.

These letters of travel cover a chapter of Phillips Brooks' life that was always of the greatest delight to him, and in which are represented many of his most striking personal characteristics. They convey not only an interesting story of travel, but also evidence of that personal charm, ready wit, and genial appreciation which those nearest to him loved so well.

"Those who have not had the good fortune to hear Phillips Brooks will be surprised with this glimpse of what must have been a delightful character."—*Academy.*

"The principal charm of the late Bishop Brooks' letters lies in their perfect unconsciousness."—*Spectator.*

Sermons. By Right Rev. Phillips Brooks. Containing Twenty Sermons. Entirely distinct from the volume of Macmillan's entitled, "Twenty Sermons." Crown 8vo, cloth, 379 pp., 6s.

The Life with God. By Right Rev. Phillips Brooks. Address to Business Men. Neat artistic wrapper, 28 pp., 6d. net; post free, 7d.

"It is almost overwhelming in its power, eloquence, and tender pleading. It is also essentially human, as is the religion which it sets forth. The preacher's great point is that the religious is the only natural and complete life."—*Christian World.*

LONDON: H. R. ALLENSON, 30, PATERNOSTER ROW, E.C.

H. R. ALLENSON'S BOOKS
FOR PREACHERS AND TEACHERS.

Sermons to Boys and Girls. By Rev. John Eames, B.A. Crown 8vo, cloth, 3s. 6d. *Just out.*

The contents of this thoroughly fresh volume are as follows:—The Story of a Runaway Slave—A Little Child shall Lead—The Boy Jesus—Under Authority—Appointed unto a Kingdom—Covetousness—The Greatest Victor and the Greatest Conquest—Silent Voices—The Children's Future—The History of a Lie—God heard the Voice of the Lad—Above Suspicion—Faithfulness—For the Sake of my Brothers and my Playmates—The Narrow Way. With Complete Index of Anecdotes, Subjects, and Illustrations.

"Mr. Eames takes pains to be interesting, and uses sensible illustrations."—*Christian World.*

"Are examples of what children's sermons ought to be, simple in language, pointed in teaching."—*Methodist Times.*

New Book by the Author of "A Box of Nails."

Tin Tacks for Tiny Folks, and other Outline Addresses for Teachers, Preachers, and Christian Workers amongst the Young. By Rev. Charles Edwards. Neat cloth, crown 8vo, 2s. 6d.

"With such a book, no preacher need fear the toil of adding to his sermon—a word to the children."—*Free Methodist.*

"These outline addresses, simple in their divisions, apt in illustration, and telling in application, will be found full of suggestion and help to teachers and superintendents."—*Sunday School Chronicle.*

Talks to Young Folks. By G. Howard James. Crown 8vo, 2s. 6d. Complete Index to Anecdotes and Subjects.

"Simple, homely language; telling illustration."—*Christian Commonwealth.*

What Shall I Tell the Children? By Rev. George V. Reichel, M.A. Crown 8vo, 5s. *A New Volume of Object Sermons.*

"Very useful to those who have to preach to children. Its merit is that t has freshness."—*British Weekly.*

The Good God ("Le Bon Dieu"). Twenty-six Five-Minute Addresses to Children. By the Rev. Bernard J. Snell, M.A., B.Sc. Crown 8vo, neat cloth, price 2s.

"Charming addresses to children, simple, homely, childlike instructions."—*Newcastle Daily Chronicle.*

"Pervaded with warmth, kindliness, and sympathy."—*South London Press.*

"Clearly and forcibly impresses his meaning on his little auditors."—*Lloyd's News.*

"Bright and vigorous, full of stories drawn from a wide range, not seldom touched with humour."—*Manchester Guardian.*

The Captain on the Bridge. By Newton Jones. A large collection of Outlines of Addresses by the Sunday School Union's Children's Evangelist. Illustrated with numerous diagrams. Small 4to, strong cloth, 2s. net; post free, 2s. 3d.

"A very helpful and suggestive book."—*Rev. Thomas Spurgeon.*

Arrows for the King's Archers. By Rev. Henry W. Little. Analytic Outline Addresses upon Religious, Temperance, and Social Topics. Crown 8vo, cloth, 3s. 6d.

Revival Sermons in Outline. By Rev. C. H. Perren. With Thoughts, Themes and Plans, by Eminent Pastors and Evangelists. Crown 8vo, cloth, 3s. 6d.

"A large number of Sermon Outlines adapted for Revival Services. Outlines gleaned from those whom God has used and owned in the blessed work."—*Sunday School Chronicle.*

"One great merit, they are brief."—*Daily Chronicle.*

"Famous sermons all passed through a capable condenser."—*Expository Times.*

"Teems with excellent suggestions."—*Christian Age.*

"To young men desirous of engaging in evangelistic work, we can highly recommend this volume."—*Methodist Times.*

LONDON: H. R. ALLENSON, 30, PATERNOSTER ROW, E.C.

STUDY AND DEVOTION.

Gospel Problems: and their Solution.
Being an enquiry into the origin of the Four Gospels, by Joseph Palmer. Crown 8vo, cloth, **6s.**

Thoughts on Prayer. By Dr. Boyd Carpenter
(Bishop of Ripon). Fcap. 8vo, cloth, **1s. 6d.**
Contents: Necessity of Prayer—Times Adverse to Prayer—Heartwork in Prayer—Reality of Answers to Prayer—Efficacy of Prayer, etc.

"It deals with many important questions. Cannot but prove helpful to all who may bestow any attention upon them. We accord this volume a most hearty welcome."—*Rock.*

Footprints of the Saviour. By Dr. Boyd
Carpenter (Bishop of Ripon). Chapters on places visited by our Lord:—Bethlehem—Cana—Sychar—Nazareth—Capernaum—Gennesaret—Decapolis—Bethany—Gethsemane—Calvary—Emmaus—Olivet. Crown 8vo, cloth, **2s. 6d.** New Edition with Thirteen Illustrations printed separately on Art Studio paper.
A very handsome gift-book and useful withal.

"Great lessons from the Life of Christ, grouped round the cities in which He did His mighty works, told here simply for simple folks. A new edition of a foremost favourite of the sick-room or prayer-meeting."—*Expository Times.*
"We are glad to observe this new edition. The treatment is mostly devotional."—*Church Review.*
"An interesting and profitable book, by the Bishop of Ripon."—*Methodist Recorder.*

Chart of the Public Life of Christ. By Rev.
J. C. Kephart, M.A. Most Valuable Accompaniment to the Gospels. Sixteen pages of Letterpress and Coloured Chart printed on strong bond paper, all neatly folded into a handy book for the pocket. Cloth limp, **2s. 6d.**
Arranged to show at a glance the events of our Lord's life, accompanied by a Coloured Diagram and a Harmony of the Four Gospels.

"There are evidences of great care. Mr. Kephart's book will be very useful."—*American Sunday School Times.*

A Catechism on the Teaching of Jesus.
By Rev. G. Currie Martin, M.A., B.D. About God, Himself, The Holy Spirit, Prayer and Worship, The Kingdom of God, our Duty, Discipleship, Sin, His own Death, His Resurrection and Second Coming, His Mission. In the words of Scripture (Revised Version). For use in Schools and Bible Classes. 16 pages, stout wrapper, clear type, **1d.**; cloth, **2d.** Post free, 2½d.

Rev. Dr. Clifford says: "This Catechism is one of the best I have seen. The questions are most skilfully arranged, and the answers are apt and effective. A better catechetical guide for the young in acquiring a knowledge of the teaching of Jesus I cannot imagine."
Professor W. F. Adeney says: "I hope indeed it may be of good service. What a grand total of teaching."
Rev. Alfred Rowland says: "I like your Catechism; I hope it may have a large circulation. The idea of stating essential Christian truths in the very words of the Founder of the Christian Religion is not only excellent in itself, but is well carried out."

Prayers and Praises: a Series of Responsive Services
for use in Sunday Schools and at Christian Endeavour Meetings. Compiled by W. B. Briant. Small 4to, 40 pages, stout paper wrapper, **2d.** In cloth, **3d.** Postage ½d. extra.

Rev. Dr. Forsyth, M.A., writes: "It seems to serve its purpose well."
Rev. B. J. Snell, M.A., writes: "I like your responsive services: the help to keep the children's minds alert and their hearts solemn."
Rev. W. J. Dawson, M.A., writes: "Admirable in form."
Rev. Dr. John Hunter writes: "Your little book is excellent in every way."

LONDON: H. R. ALLENSON, 30, PATERNOSTER ROW, E.C.

WHAT TOPIC SHALL I TAKE?

JUST OUT. By the Editor of "The Tool Basket."

Illustrations and Incidents. For Preachers, Teachers, and Christian Workers. With complete Index of subjects. Neat cloth, 1s.

"A choice and well-arranged collection of anecdotes marked by much freshness."—*Methodist Recorder.*

The Tool Basket for Preachers, Sunday-School Teachers, and Open-Air Workers. Being a Collection of 300 Sermon Outlines, Pegs of Thought, Sunday-school Addresses, etc. Twenty-fifth Thousand. Strong limp cloth boards, narrow 8vo, 1s.

The Seed Basket. 300 Outlines for Ministers, Sunday-school Teachers, and Christian Endeavourers. Cloth, 1s. By the Compiler of the "Tool Basket," now in its Twenty-fifth Thousand.

The above three useful little Books are now to be obtained in one volume, entitled—

Outlines and Illustrations. For Preachers, Teachers, and Christian Workers, comprising SIX HUNDRED Outlines and 250 Illustrative Anecdotes. Neat cloth, 2s. 6d. It thus forms a veritable vade-mecum.

Object Sermons in Outline. Forty-five Topics for Children and P.S.A.'s. By Rev. C. H. Tyndall, D.D. Crown 8vo, 3s. 6d.

It is worth while to point out that if it is not possible or convenient to employ the object accompanying the text, these addresses and outlines of addresses of Dr. Tyndall's are so arranged that by means of a slight description which is given in every case the actual object can be dispensed with.

The Expository Times speaks of this book as the "Great Kindergarten in the pulpit."

A Box of Nails for Busy Christian Workers. 160 Bible Readings and Outline Addresses. By Rev. C. Edwards. Crown 8vo, 1s. 6d. Second Edition, Sixth Thousand.

"Display real ingenuity and aptness. Strongly advise the investment."—*Primitive Methodist.*
"Sure to be of service."—*Literary World.*

Seed Corn for the Sower. By Rev. C. H. Perren. A Book of Illustrations for the Pulpit and Platform. With Complete Indices to Subjects, Texts and Authors quoted. Cloth boards, 394 pp., 5s.

| "Hard-pressed speakers will often find here what the are in need of."—*Christian World.*
"A boon to Preachers and Teachers."—*Methodist Times.*

The Open Secret; or, the Bible Explaining Itself. By Hannah Whitall Smith. Nineteen Bible Readings by the Author of "The Christian's Secret of a Happy Life." Crown 8vo, 326 pp., sewed, 2s. 6d. A series of stimulating studies.

Which Bible to Read. Revised or Authorised? A Statement of Facts, and an Appeal to the Modern Christian. By Rev. Frank Ballard, M.A. Fcap. 8vo, neat cloth, 1s. net; post free, 1s. 2d. New, revised, and much enlarged Edition. Crown 8vo, 3s. 6d.

"Very useful. It is a very great advantage that you deal with the Old Testament."—*Rev. Dr. Westcott, Bishop of Durham.*

LONDON: H. R. ALLENSON, 30, PATERNOSTER ROW, E.C.

TRACTS FOR THE TIMES.

"Are admirable for putting into the hands of thoughtful young people."—*Scottish Endeavour*.

The Spirit of Dives. By the Rev. C. Silvester Horne, M.A. An Indictment of Indifference. 1d.; post free, 1½d. (Tracts for the Times, No. 1.)
"An earnest sermon, marked by frankness and wisdom."—*Literary World*.

The Sobriety of Hope. By the Rev. C. Silvester Horne, M.A. 1d.; post free, 1½d. (Tracts for the Times, No. 6.)
"A delightful address in praise of optimism."—*New Age*.

Foundations. By Rev. Herbert W. Horwill. 1d.; post free, 1½d. (Tracts for the Times, No. 7.)
"Emphasises the distinction between a Foundation and a Founder. Warns against the misleading influences of tradition, both as regards the Bible and the interpretation of its teaching, and urges parents and teachers to be careful not to give erroneous impressions of the meaning of Scripture to their children, which may afterwards have to be painfully unlearned."—*British Friend*.

The Duty of Being Young. By the Rev. J. H. Jowett, M.A. 1d.; post free, 1½d. Address to Guild and C. E. Members. (Tracts for the Times, No. 4.)

Am I Fit to Take the Lord's Supper? By Rev. Samuel Pearson. 16 pp., crown 8vo, 1d.; post free, 1½d. 6s. per 100. (Tracts for the Times, No. 5.) *15th Thousand*.
"Just the thing to give to backward disciples. It would be good for presidents to give these little books to all the active members in their societies who are not yet church members."—*Scottish Endeavour*.

Citizenship and Its Duties. By Rev. Bernard J. Snell, M.A., B.Sc. A Sermon. "Apathy is the Enemy." Crown 8vo, 16 pp., 1d.; post free, 1½d. (Tracts for the Times, No. 3.)

Why are we Independents? By Rev. Bernard J. Snell, M.A., B.Sc. Sermon preached on Free Church Sunday. Crown 8vo, 2d.; post free, 2½d. (Tracts for the Times, No. 8.)

Human Body, The, and How to Take Care of It. By Wm. E. Lee, M.R.C.S.E. A Tract for the People. An Address delivered to the Fulham Y.M.C.A. Crown 8vo, 22 pages, 2d.; post free, 2½d.
"An admirable tract."—*Christian*.

The Happy Warrior. By Rev. Dr. Forsyth, M.A. A Sermon preached as a Memorial Sermon upon the late Mr. W. E. Gladstone. Crown 8vo, 32 pages, 3d.; post free, 3½d.
A fine, inspiring address to young people.

Christianity and Art. By Rev. William Pierce (Tracts for the Times No. 2). 16 pages, 1d.; post free, 1½d.

Nonconformist Minister's Ordinal, The. A fresh setting of the Preachers' Services for Baptismal, Marriage, and Funeral Services. **Large Type.**

Fcap. 8vo, neat cloth, 1s. net; postage 2d. extra.
Dark red cloth, 1s. 3d. net. ditto.
Black buckram, very strong, 1s. 6d. net. ditto.
Turkey morocco, 3s. 9d. net. ditto.

This book will go comfortably into a breast pocket.
"Judicious and devout."—*Presbyterian*.
"A work many Nonconformist Ministers will be glad to possess. It is handily and tastefully presented."—*Literary World*.

LONDON: H. R. ALLENSON, 30, PATERNOSTER ROW, E.C.

FROM AMERICAN PREACHERS.

The Coming People. By Charles F. Dole. Fcap. 8vo, 5s. A social and religious study of life from the standpoint of the beatitude, "The meek shall inherit the earth."

"Is as sincere in logic as it is inspiring in cheer and hope."—*Boston Herald.*

The **Spectator** devoted its leading article to this book, and said:—"This is a healthy and virile essay, which the reader will be thankful to Mr. Dole for having given him. There are in the book the outlines of ideas of which we shall probably hear a good deal in the future as the attempt to interpret the Christian world and the Christian spirit in terms of the modern doctrine of evolution becomes more developed."

"It is distinctly refreshing to read this book, written in a style quite admirable, and under the impulse of a generous and reverent spirit. This book ought to be widely read, and we are sure that he who begins the work will finish it. Mr. Dole has the insight that discerns principles, and a keen eye for facts."—*Methodist Recorder.*

"Dealing with great problems, it is manly, simple, and invigorating."—*The Inquirer.*

Christianity between Sundays. By Rev. Dr. George Hodges. Sermons. Handsome cloth, crown 8vo, 3s. 6d.

Heresy of Cain. By Rev. Dr. George Hodges. Sermons. Handsome cloth, crown 8vo, 3s. 6d.

From Things to God. By David H. Greer, D.D. Sermons. Crown 8vo, cloth, 6s.

Christ at the Door of the Heart, and other Sermons. By Rev. Morgan Dix, D.D., Rector of Holy Trinity, New York. Crown 8vo, cloth, 363 pp., 3s. 6d.

The Spirit of the Age. By Rev. D. J. Burrell, D.D. Thirty-seven Sermons. Large crown 8vo, 5s. The subjects are brightly and vigorously treated.

Social Meanings of Religious Experiences. By Rev. G. D. Herron, D.D. Crown 8vo, cloth, 3s. 6d.

"Dr. Herron is a fearless preacher of Righteousness. The note struck is sufficiently evident from the title of the book."—From a full-page review in the *New Age.*

The *Review of Reviews* in a full-page notice credited this work of Dr. Herron's as the Book of the Month.

The Christian Society. By Rev. G. D. Herron, D.D. With Introduction by Dr. Charles A. Berry (late Chairman of the Congregational Union). Crown 8vo, cloth, 3s. 6d.

"Never in our day have we had the moral foundations and spiritual law of a Christian Society preached with such prophetic fervour and power as in this volume."—*Christian World.*

The New Redemption. By Rev. G. D. Herron, D.D. A Call to the Church to re-construct Society according to the Gospel of Christ. Fcap. 8vo, cloth, 3s. 6d. Sixth Thousand.

"A book to be read and pondered."—*American Independent.*

A Plea for the Gospel. By Rev. G. D. Herron, D.D. Fcap. 8vo, cloth, 3s. 6d.

"Thoughtful people may well pay heed to Dr. Herron, who in sincerity and impetuous zeal bids fair to be a second Luther."—*Boston Beacon.*

The Christian State. By Rev. G. D. Herron, D.D. A Political Vision of Christ. Fcap. 8vo, cloth, 3s. 6d.

"Mr. Herron is a man of power. He writes with immense enthusiasm and fine culture. Mr. Herron, like a prophet—a speaker of God, that he is—does not argue; he appeals to one's moral nature; he pleads, he commands."—From the *New York Critic.*

LONDON: H. R. ALLENSON, 30, PATERNOSTER ROW, E.C.

www.ingramcontent.com/pod-product-compliance
Lightning Source LLC
Chambersburg PA
CBHW030306170426
43202CB00009B/892